Pam LaManna
(574) 850-5090

Nothing in All creation can
separate you from My Love.
Jesus
God
Holy Spirit 3:17
Jesus
always

D1277786

Chit Happens

March 18, 2023

Pam,
I am honored to meet you
May you live in the love of God
always

Norene

Chit Happens

A Guide to Discovering Divinity

NARAIN ISHAYA

BALBOA.
PRESS

A DIVISION OF HAY HOUSE

Balboa Press books may be ordered through booksellers or by contacting:

Balboa Press
A Division of Hay House
1663 Liberty Drive
Bloomington, IN 47403
www.balboapress.com
1-(877) 407-4847

Because of the dynamic nature of the Internet, any web addresses or
links contained in this book may have changed since publication and
may no longer be valid. The views expressed in this work are solely those
of the author and do not necessarily reflect the views of the publisher,
and the publisher hereby disclaims any responsibility for them.

The author of this book does not dispense medical advice or prescribe
the use of any technique as a form of treatment for physical, emotional,
or medical problems without the advice of a physician, either directly
or indirectly. The intent of the author is only to offer information
of a general nature to help you in your quest for emotional and
spiritual well-being. In the event you use any of the information in
this book for yourself, which is your constitutional right, the author
and the publisher assume no responsibility for your actions.

Certain stock imagery © Thinkstock.
Any people depicted in stock imagery provided by Thinkstock are
models, and such images are being used for illustrative purposes only.

ISBN: 978-1-4525-5819-6 (e)
ISBN: 978-1-4525-5820-2 (sc)
ISBN: 978-1-4525-5821-9 (hc)

Library of Congress Control Number: 2012916285

Printed in the United States of America

Balboa Press rev. date: 9/24/2012

To my Teacher, Krishnananda…
thank you for coming back to get me.

To all beings from all traditions, past, present and future,
who have made the Kingdom of Heaven second to nothing.

p. 35-37 my peace/wisdom

xprayer

p. 170 divine will no karma yes ☺

p. 89, 91, 99 -101, 103

p. 34 we become free when we
repent & forgive.

p. 173 7 churches / chakras

p. 83
#99
"the present"
"you are free"

" *To penetrate the mysteries, to bless with a good conscience, to be great and yet empty, to return to Stillness and be forgiving, to be compassionate and to deliver all people, to do good deeds and help people reach the other shore — these are the great benefits of our path of cultivation. To calm people in stormy times, to help them understand the nature of things, to maintain purity, to nourish all things, to respect all life, and to answer the needs of those whose beliefs come from the heart.* "

From *The Jesus Sutras* by Martin Palmer

CONTENTS

PREFACE

Many people have said to me over my life that they could see me writing a book. I always thought that I would write one too, but how do you do that? What do you write that hasn't been written a thousand times before? I have had articles published and written for various websites and publications, but a book just seemed too big a task, so I just conveniently forgot about it.

Then, a couple of years ago my spiritual teacher said to me, "Narain, I want you to write a book. It would be great if it was in question and answer format so that it's easy to read, but clearly shows the path of waking up."

"Yes," I said, because that is what I always say when he asks me to do something!

At the time, I was travelling a lot giving seminars, workshops and retreats. These provided fertile ground for the questions. With some live recording, and some, no doubt flawed memory, the content of the book began to take shape. Very quickly, it was evident there was more than enough for a book. That was easy!

Then came the process of taking the spoken word and making it the written word. That was not so easy!

Pouring over the content, removing repeated questions, or answers; trying to have a coherent thread of meaning for the chapters; it all took a lot longer than it seemed like it was going to.

What began as a co-authored project became a solo project and has morphed and changed and changed again. It has had a life of its own, and when I was actually surrendered to doing it, it *was* easy.

I have learned a lot through this process. I have learned that spoken words need a little help to get on a page and make sense. I have learned that the universe has much more patience for me than I have for myself. I have learned that, for most people, being committed no matter what is the most rare of things; that the mind will always offer a seemingly valid reason why you should quit, and it is a lie.

I have learned that I *can* write a book, and the next one will not take so long.

So, my teacher, I have done what you asked me to do. I am sure if I ever write an autobiography, the only apt title would be, "Better late than never." If the autobiography never comes, then maybe it should be my headstone!

The text of this book has come from live dialogue and teaching from the past several years. It covers many topics, ultimately revealing the possibility for anyone to walk the timeless path of the mystic, without needing to leave behind the fulfilling experience of life.

It can be read from front to back in traditional book form, or opened at any page for a little reminder and inspiration for anyone who wants to know the fullness of who they are, and the simplicity of discovering that.

There are a few references in this book to the Ishayas and their teaching. The word *Isha* is a Sanskrit word which means, among other things, "highest consciousness." The ending −*ya* means "for." The Ishayas are a group of people who have dedicated their lives to experiencing the highest consciousness they can, and sharing the possibility of that with all who are ready and willing to hear.

They have a meditation that is called *Ascension*. It is a mechanical, belief free system that is incredibly effective at helping anyone transcend the mind. There is more about the teaching of Ascension in the epilogue to this book.

The word **'*Chit*'** is Sanskrit for consciousness itself, and the title is a play on a popular Western saying.

ACKNOWLEDGEMENTS

Maharishi, it is impossible to put into words the gratitude I have for your guidance, your presence, your constant and selfless example of service and commitment to the awakening of humanity…and in my case, your patience!

My beautiful wife, Satta, your constant and boundless love, your total commitment to Truth, and your inability to see me, or anyone for that matter, as small has been the greatest gift to my life. Also, your innocent fascination with a world of sleeping Gods brings me endless Joy.

To my mother Lesley, to Jenny, Lachlan, Ruth and Chloe, for loving me and supporting me to the fulfilment of a dream that was burning from the beginning, even when you didn't understand. I cannot begin to express my Love and gratitude for everything you have done, and continue to do, for me.

And Dad. I wish you could have held the book, but I know you know what's in it. Thank you for giving me this life. It is a truly amazing experience.

A big thank you also to Adriane from Balboa. After all my questions to you, you deserve a raise…or a medal…or both!

To all of you around the world who are consciously seeking a way to wake up, thank you. For those of you who have taken the plunge and learned to Ascend, thank you. Every time you use these sacred techniques, you bring yourself, and consequently all of humanity, closer to the realization of freedom.

Lastly, to those immortal beings who have always shown up at the right time so that I would clearly see the doubts in my mind as futile ghosts. Your teaching is the real thing and it is an honour to be a part of it. I pray that my best has been good enough.

INTRODUCTION

Throughout recorded history, the majority of humanity has had a relationship with the Divine that is completely external. Not only has God been seen as something external and separate, but also, through that perceived distance, God has been a place to project all of the darkest parts of our collective personality.

In all cultures God is called Love, and yet for virtually every one of us, the image we have been fed of the Divine is actually anything but loving. God is described as wrathful, jealous, angry, and punishing, a being to be feared and obeyed.

There have always been those who have had a different relationship with God, one that is subjective. Sometimes during our long history, these have been a few scattered individuals solely sharing the experience of the Divine within with anyone who was ready and willing to hear. At other times, they were lesser-known mystical adepts, existing within the confines of established religions. At other times still, whole societies at large have known this most universal of truths: that the Kingdom of Heaven is within.

Over the millennia, through the myriad of experiences available on this planet, the collective consciousness of humanity has been slowly (painfully slowly) evolving. As a result of this evolution, the old ideas and projections of the Divine are beginning to undo. The understanding that eternal peace is a subjective *choice* is becoming more and more widespread, more and more acceptable.

At this time, there is an unprecedented awakening occurring for the human race. In what, in the grand scheme of things, is the blink of an omnipotent eye, people are beginning to search for teachings and tools that will allow them to take their awareness inward, beyond the surface of the mind, to a direct experience of their True Nature as Divinity itself. There is a growing sense that living a life of separation and suffering is not necessary.

Many teachings have appeared to answer this awakening, some new, some ancient. Of these, some actually have the means to fulfill life's purpose of union with God. Most do not. Like children fumbling in the dark, mankind is looking for a way to return to the light.

The path of return has existed forever. The Teaching is actually clearly laid out in all traditions for those with the eyes to see. All of the greatest teachers of history taught the same thing in different ways. They all knew that eternal peace lies within the heart of every human, that separation and suffering and death are the sad dreams of the lost, sleeping children of God.

This book is unique in that not only have I been able to share my experience and perspectives of the eternal dance of consciousness, but also, it has as its conclusion a direct invitation to a real Teaching, the sole purpose of which is the awakening of humanity.

My hopes for this book are many. May it enliven your desire to wake up, or intensify that desire at whatever stage it is already kindled. May it answer questions you have had, whether or not you knew you had them. May it undo many of the common spiritual concepts that, no matter how beautiful, ultimately distract the aspirant from the true goal of human life. May it let you know that the path to freedom can be easy, swift, and joyful. May you, at the end of this text, have had at least a glimpse of your own magnificent potential.

CHAPTER 1

Truth is Universal

It is a fascinating thing that over the millennia, the search for our true nature has become embroiled in mysticism and complexity. For something to be called Truth it must be universal, equally present for all everywhere, forever. Unfortunately for most of us, the search for Truth has become something that is seen as difficult and reserved for only a select few.

This cannot be the case. Truth cannot be only for some. It cannot be in some places and not in others. It must be omnipresent, and it must be now. Not only that, but it must be simple, the most simple of things. How can it be difficult to realize that which you already are? The discovery of Absolute Truth must only be a matter of learning to discriminate that which you *are* from that which you are *not*. This discrimination is a valid spiritual path, *the* spiritual path if what you want is to awaken from the dream of separation and limitation. Luckily it is also the simplest, fastest, and most enjoyable path as well. Who would even want to undertake such a journey if it were joyless? The fact is, it is the ultimate Joy.

The path of awareness and self-realization, otherwise known as enlightenment, is as equally available to a housewife in Minnesota as a yogi in the Himalayas. In fact, the journey may be easier for the former simply because of the lack of spiritual concepts in the average Minnesotan housewife. The only requirement is the desire to be free, and the willingness to go for it whole-heartedly.

The greatest Teachers of history have clearly shown the universal nature of Truth. All described the same reality; all taught the simplicity of return. Any complexity in the teaching came from those who followed, the ones who knew only the letter, rather than the spirit, of the Teaching. Spiritual concepts and beliefs serve only to mask the omnipresent splendor of our own divine light.

It is our concepts and beliefs that are the root cause of all separation, all pain and all suffering. While these beliefs are unconsciously mistaken for Truth, we will only live in the world as we believe it to be, rather than the world as it is. Once these beliefs are clearly seen, and with a valid way to surrender them to something greater, there is no boundary that cannot be transcended; none. The True Nature of reality cannot be understood, nor conceptualized; it can only be directly experienced. It is an open invitation to all to return to their birthright of eternal peace, limitless joy, and boundless creative potential.

1. What is God?

The word God is simply a word. It is used here to refer to the absolute source of all experience. Beyond all form and appearance there is a field of limitless, silent awareness devoid of all movement and change. The discovery of this field as a direct experience is the purpose of spiritual practice.

All cultures have a word for the experience of this awareness. In India it is sometimes referred to Turiya, the fourth state of consciousness beyond waking, sleeping and dreaming. In Japan it has been known as Satori. Early Christians called it "the peace that passeth all understanding," as the mind cannot grasp it, yet it can absolutely be experienced. It has been called the Tao, Silence, Stillness, Presence, the Absolute, pure consciousness, infinite love and endless peace.

While the words are many, the experience is one. While the paths to the discovery of it may be many, the experience is subjective, and comes only from letting go of the attachment to, and identification with, the mind. Meditation is invaluable for correcting one's relationship to the mind, and allowing the discovery of the presence that lies beyond.

As the experience of the silent presence grows, it reveals itself to be so all encompassing, so utterly all-consuming, that the word God simply points to the magnitude of it.

Many of the world's religious teachings have portrayed the Divine as something outside of you, something to be feared and obeyed. This is not God's fault. God has been given a bad rap by humanity's ignorance of spiritual truth.

Whatever word is used to describe limitless awareness is inadequate. This is about the direct inner realization of the Divine, the remembering of your true nature. It is not about picking up beliefs, ideas or concepts. This is absolutely spiritual, but not religious or based on belief. Your freedom from limitation and suffering is all down to your own experience, your own relationship with your mind. Just beyond the chatter of the mind is the indescribable beauty of your own consciousness. Identification with that is freedom, call it what you will.

2. How can you say there is a universal truth? What is true for me may not necessarily be true for someone else.

On one level you are right, but that level is not the level of *absolute* truth, it is the level of *relative* truth. This is the level where truth or falsehood is determined by the mind. It is based on what *feels* true, which is how we formulate our beliefs. It is a level of truth that is determined by our mental filters. As much as it may not appear this way, these truths are not based entirely on experience, and so need to be defended and reinforced.

A truth at this level may appear to be true for you, but will not be true for everyone, always.

From as early as I can remember, I was always interested in spirituality. Because of where I grew up, the earliest experiences of this for me were through Christianity. I have always loved Jesus. There was something so infinitely compassionate about his example to me.

As a child, when I heard that heaven was exclusively reserved for His followers alone, it just didn't make any sense.

I asked people, "What about all the people who died before he came? What about all the people who never got to know about him? What about all the people who have their own religions?"

No one could give me a satisfactory answer, not one that seemed in alignment with what I read Jesus was actually supposed to have said.

All of the answers I was given were based on something *they* may have believed to be true, but Jesus never said it. They were told it, and just accepted it as fact. None of them seemed to have given it one moment's contemplation; none of it was based on their experience. I wasn't prepared to accept it.

Only a few short years ago I was talking with a priest, a really nice guy. He found out what I do, and with only a small personal charge said to me, "We believe that meditation is a tool of the antichrist."

I said, "For you to use the word antichrist, you must be pretty clear on what Christ is."

"Oh yes I am." He replied.

I asked, "Did Jesus really say that the Kingdom of God is within?"

"Yes, he said that," replied my new friend.

"And did Jesus say that the Kingdom Heaven is at hand?"

"Yes, he said that too."

"And did Jesus teach to anyone, including women, tax collectors and gentiles?"

"He sure did."

"So, Jesus said the Kingdom of Heaven is within you, at hand, meaning now, and it is available to all people, regardless of who they are or where they came from. I also think he said that if you stop following your mind into the past, or worrying about the future, God will be there to look after you, you will discover it for yourself. He also said something about all the things He did, you can do, and more. The opposite of that teaching, anti to that Christ would be a teaching that says the Kingdom of Heaven is reserved only for a special few, that it requires something more of you than you already are, and exists off in another point in space and time, probably after you die, if you've been good."

"Our teaching, which uses meditation as a tool, is one that says that freedom and the Kingdom of Heaven are available right here and now for anyone to experience. All you have to do is let go of the mind's ceaseless movement from past to future and back again to discover the innate divinity that you already are. It is equally present within all beings, regardless of background, culture, sex or age. Nothing is required other than the willingness to remember how to let go. There is not very much which is opposed to Christ's teaching in any of that; in fact it is absolutely in alignment with it."

He nearly fell over! He knew that his statement had been based in something he was told, and had not questioned, something that was not his experience.

Relative truth is the birthplace of all conflict. You believe one thing, I believe another, and if our beliefs clash or challenge one another in any way then one must defeat the other. How many times have great wars been fought because two sets of conflicting relative truths came up against one another? How many times has one belief system slaughtered many people trying to impose their own relative truth upon others?

There is another level of truth. This level has nothing to do with belief; it is not relative, it is absolute. It does not create divisions because it is unified.

No conflict is possible because it is not based on what you *believe* to be true, but is based upon experience. It is not dependant upon religion, background, race or behavior.

This is not about religion. This scenario plays out in every area of our lives continuously. Discovering the difference for your self as a living experience is the difference between a life lived in separation and judgment, and a life lived in permanent peace and awareness of Divinity.

Beyond all of the beliefs we hold dear, beyond all the individual positions and judgments is a field of limitless, silent awareness. This field of presence is common to all. It is the fullest experience of the present moment, and in it there is no judgment, no separation, no conflict and no suffering.

Whether you agree or disagree with what I am saying is not important. Whether you desire to find out for your self is. The experience of universal truth is yours for the asking, it is with you always.

What you call it is irrelevant. It is peace, it is stillness, it is silence, and it is God. It is less than heartbeat away for you, and everyone else, forever. It is the end of all divisions, and the birthplace of immortality. It is literally the Kingdom of Heaven.

3. What is meant by the statement, "The Kingdom of Heaven is within?"

It means that the Kingdom of Heaven, which would also infer God, is within you. It would seem from that one simple statement if you were going to seek Heaven as an experience, then it would be necessary to learn to take the awareness inward, beyond the mind. Study of theology and philosophy is fine if all you want is to know *about* the experience, or what other people think about it, or to learn what man has decided is an appropriate way to behave to be in alignment with it. But if you want to experience it for yourself, you have to go inside, because it is there, within you. It is actually not different than your own consciousness.

I once heard that statement translated from Aramaic, which went something like "The Kingdom of Heaven is of the inner and the outer." That which we seek is both within us and all around us continually, but we have been conditioned to seek something else, something spectacular, always something other than the here and now.

The ego survives on the concept of specialness. It desires to be spectacular. The truth of divinity is that it is realized as the most ordinary of states. That which is termed enlightenment is rare, but this is not because it is difficult; in fact, quite the opposite. It is rare because of its ultimate simplicity. The Jesus', Buddha's and Krishna's of the world were quite possibly the most ordinary people who have ever lived, and in that surrender to their own non-specialness, they became spectacular.

Most people miss the goal of human life because the subtlest levels of the mind are looking for the spectacular. Ego needs to be recognized as having obtained something. The limited self always wants to get something out of the experience. "What do I get out of enlightenment?" it asks. To the ego the answer is, "Nothing."

What there *is* for you is eternal peace; nothing special, just rare. What is termed "bliss" is so because it is the realization of that which was always present, the most natural of states. Christ knew full well, as does every realized being, that the exquisite experience of freedom is the recognition of the divine perfection of all that is, exactly as it exists now. Nothing needs to be fixed or improved, simply experienced. To turn the awareness inward is really to stop focusing on everything other than that.

We are continually walking through the Kingdom of Heaven, we just don't recognize it because we have become accustomed to only recognizing thoughts, feelings and sensory experiences. It is amazing really, that identification with the movements in the mind has obscured mankind's recognition of their own divinity.

This is the value of meditation, to begin to see the movements of the mind as separate from you, and from there, to take the awareness deeper into the presence of the Self. All our lives we are so involved with doing. Then, when we begin to seek for Peace, we begin doing all over again to achieve that. We go from workshop to workshop, read book after book, go to church after church, always less than a heartbeat away from the presence of God.

In all of this, what we are never taught to do, at least not effectively, is to just stop and be aware, to be still. In those moments of stillness we are opening to Presence, and by continually surrendering to that presence, it has the opportunity to claim your awareness itself, for you to return to Union with that.

It is simply identification with thought that has created the illusion of separation. To move the awareness "within" is to let go of the movement of thought, go beyond the mind and directly experience the silence that was there the whole time. When that Silence is experienced fully, it can only be termed Divine. It *is* the Kingdom of Heaven. It *is* God. It is your birthright to directly experience you are, and have always been, one with that.

Christ continually said the same thing as all great Teachers of history; what you seek you already are, it is here and now and within you…it is your own radiant awareness. Seek that with all your heart and the Kingdom of Heaven will be revealed. It was always there. We were just looking in the wrong place.

4. What is Consciousness?

At any time, you can be aware. You know you experience, and this quality could be called awareness.

Beyond that awareness is a completely non-dual state, which is infinitely alert, only to its self. It is a field of infinite possibility, eternally un-manifest, completely beyond time and space.

It is the truest experience of the Self. It has no individual qualities at all, and is the one source of all the various appearances of creation. This field is pure consciousness.

Consciousness is the root of the universe, as quantum physics is discovering. Without consciousness there is no experience of the universe. The universe, and everything in it, cannot exist independent of consciousness, but consciousness needs nothing to exist; it is existence.

It is consciousness that, when it becomes identified with individual perception, believes its self to be the limited "me" rather than the infinite, universal "I."

Consciousness is the Self of all things, the life essence of everything in creation, without exception. Consciousness is the unified field, the level at which all things are one.

It is what sees through your eyeballs, hears through your ears and feels with your senses. It is the part of you that cannot be hurt or injured in any way and is not subject to birth or death. It, in fact, is you...the real you. It is your life's purpose to remember that, to return to your natural state of infinite being-ness.

You are the essence of creation, the infinite possibility of the Divine. You have forgotten that. You believe that you are a little, individual being with no power or choice in what you are. This is not true, no matter how much you believe it. You are endlessly free, and it's time you remembered that. It's time you came home.

5. What is Enlightenment?

Enlightenment is the direct experience that formless consciousness is all there is, and you *are* that. This state, however, is a concept for most people. A more appropriate question would be, "If you could have anything at all right now, any wish granted, what would that be?" Many people would ask for more money, or better health, or a better relationship. All of these things are worthy and deserved, but what is it that these wishes would give to you?

In a moment of honesty, you can see that if you had more money, a better job, a better relationship or health then you would experience more love, freedom, happiness, joy or peace. At the root of every human desire is the desire to experience these things: Happiness, Joy, Peace, love and Freedom. Unfortunately, humanity has sacrificed the goal to the pursuit of the things that we *think* will deliver it to us.

Once you have begun the earnest search for freedom, the mind actually needs you to continually be looking for the next thing in order for it to survive. Habitually, we don't want to surrender the thing we desire to the experience that we are looking for. From this perspective, it is always desire that we are seeking to fulfill, and desires are endless.

If we believe that we desire a new car, and we work and work and finally get it, we feel the sense of satisfaction, the achievement. Soon afterwards, however, we begin to seek the next thing to fulfill us.

The freedom we experience is never from obtaining the car, or the thing we wanted. It is always because, in the moment we fulfill the desire, the desire itself is surrendered. There is a moment (or several moments) where there is no desire, and consequently, what remains is freedom.

When all attachment to personal desire is surrendered, awareness can open to this moment. In that, there is no concept of a separate, limited me. There is only the limitless contentment of Now. This is the doorway to enlightenment.

6. What is ignorance?

You could say that ignorance is the opposite of enlightenment. It is, as the word suggests, the ignoring of something. It is the ignoring of Truth. In a spiritual context, it is ignoring the presence and sovereignty of the Divine.

The mind loves to point the finger to the outside and complain about how unfair life is. It will give you a million reasons why fear and judgment are justified. The ego believes itself to be separate from Love and needs this version of reality to be supported by you to so it remains in control.

In order to believe that darkness is the only reality you must invest a lot of effort to continue to turn away from the Sun. You must remain focused on your shadow. We do this all the time with consciousness. We invest all of our energy in focusing on judgments in order to ignore the light of consciousness in our experience.

It seems strange at first to hear that ignorance is a moment-by-moment choice. It has become so much our experience that it seems like it is the natural state. This does not mean that it is. It is only a habit, and with perseverance, any habit can be broken.

This is the purpose of spiritual practice. It breaks the habit of ignorance. All that is required is the willingness to begin. You have to be willing to give up anything that keeps you in separation. Any belief, any judgment that keeps you away from absolute peace will at some point have to be surrendered. This is the easiest of things by the way. It only becomes difficult if you want to hang on to the belief more than you want to be free, and this is your choice. It is also the height of ignorance.

7. If truth is universal, why is religion at the center of much of the world's conflict?

It is a good point that religion is at the core of much of the world's conflict. There is an important line to draw between religion and spirituality. Religion is based on dogma and intellectual understanding of a spiritual message. It is the interpretation of a message rather than a direct experience of the underlying truth.

Spirituality is an intimate, organic and constantly new journey into Truth, into the experience of inner presence.

It is the discovery and exploration of the realm of consciousness. No knowledge is required, no certificates or levels are gained, and none are excluded except by their own choice. All are equal on this quest.

The absolute reality needs no defense or justification, and nobody's peace is better or worse than anyone else's. The direct experience of the perfect silence that lies beyond the mind is the antidote to all conflict. No theology has any weight there.

It comes as a shock to many religious people to hear that Jesus was actually not a Christian, that Buddha was actually not a Buddhist. They were exponents of the spiritual flavor of their particular time and place, and yet all had a burning desire to know themselves. All discovered the same reality; that the Kingdom of Heaven, the Buddha nature, and the Supreme God are the same thing.

The religions that have sprung up in their names bare little resemblance to the original teachings. The basis of the major religions of the world were put together on the unfortunate misunderstanding of, and sometimes the outright desire to hide, the messages of the original Teachers. These theologies were often completed hundreds of years after the passing of the original Teacher. It is all quite bizarre really.

I am not saying religion doesn't have its place, it does. It is, however, primarily a social phenomenon. For the soul desiring true freedom, it does not offer a path. Even amidst the changes, mistranslations and misinterpretations, there is enough of the original message left to know that what I am saying is true. The Jesus', Buddhas and all awakened Teachers of history are an invitation to become as they were. They serve as the way-showers to enlightenment. Not one of them said that they were here to do it for us. This is not possible. Each being that discovers the ultimate reality, shows us that we can make the journey for ourselves, but do it ourselves we must.

Reality is One. The Kingdom of Heaven is within, and it is now. It is universal, and it is your birthright. It exists forever, closer than your next breath, waiting patiently for you to recognize it for yourself.

8. If there is an ultimate subjective reality, then why is it so rarely recognized?

Where is that reality even talked about? There *are* places, but they are few and far between. As a result, discovering true freedom is not something most people have even heard is possible.

Society in general is founded on the principle that your happiness depends upon something outside of you, and that your value is based upon what you have accumulated, also existing outside of you. This is the first problem. How much time can you have for discovering the ultimate reality and true freedom when you need a new kitchen, or to drop a few dress sizes in order to feel good about yourself?

Even with spirituality, the ultimate reality is, again, placed outside of you. Your worthiness of your birthright is based in how you have behaved and what you have done, and will be revealed to you somewhere else in space and time after you die, if you have been good.

All of our attention is focused on the transient. Everything in modern society focuses the attention on everything other than the one thing that matters.

It is quite obvious too, that most people are more interested in which celebrity happens to be dancing on ice this week, or what game happens to be on television next, or who wore the same dress better at the awards show, than discovering eternal peace.

It seems to be a question of spiritual maturity. Why does one person thirst for truth and another not? I don't know. I do know that for me there was a constant background of urgency throughout my entire life. I didn't know exactly what it was, but it was always there.

I was always interested in spirituality, and yet there was a knowingness that no matter what I found or read or heard, that there was something really important missing.

I had huge problems committing to anything, because I was waiting for the path to God to present itself.

For no apparent reason at all, one day I woke up and it was like the lights had come on for the first time. All of a sudden there was the knowingness that I was here to discover union with God as a living experience. I still didn't know how, but I knew it had to happen. Magically, almost within hours, a good friend of mine handed me a book that helped me to know that this was possible. I started to find people who could help me move towards the goal.

No matter what I did, no matter what meditation I tried, or healing modality I learned, the gap between what those things were offering and the desire for awakening became greater. As beautiful as the things I was doing were, they were not going to bring enlightenment, and yet I kept on going.

As the desire for freedom intensified, the path became clearer and eventually a teaching was revealed that could bring me, and anyone else for that matter, home.

From the very beginning using that meditation, a presence began to be apparent. That presence revealed itself to be an infinitely aware silence without end. The practice I had learned allowed me to easily and continuously prioritize that presence. It allowed for the surrendering of the limited individual self to a greater and greater experience of wholeness.

How many of my friends at the time walked that path? None. How many of the people that I knew wanted a subjective experience of their own divinity? Almost none. Why do people care more about a plastic, Hollywood version of life rather than a direct experience of limitless consciousness? Who knows?

I do know that when the desire is kindled within you, the path reveals itself. For everyone who sincerely desires true freedom, the universe will move to bring it to them. For everyone who realizes the goal and discovers his or her true nature, it becomes more apparent for everyone else. That's the power of the path, that's the beauty of it.

9. Do the experiences of the Christian mystics have anything in common with the sages of the ancient Eastern traditions?

The experience of the Absolute is common to all. The path to its realization, however, can be very different. The presence of truth is absolute and all encompassing. If Jesus and Buddha and Krishna showed up at the same dinner party there would be no conflict, I'm sure. Maybe a few words of greeting exchanged or knowing smiles as the Silence recognizes itself in the other, but no conflict. All conflict is born in the mind.

The idea that my way is better than your way, or that only by being born in a particular culture are you qualified to be free, is all ego. It has no relevance to the Absolute. All humans in all cultures at all times are qualified simply because they exist. Divinity is all, and all is Divine.

Anyone with the sincere desire and willingness to go for it will discover the ultimate reality for themselves. It is inevitable. The path walked by many of the Christian mystics is riddled with pain. Many of them would have great experiences of consciousness, and then it would dissolve into the *learned* reality of pain and suffering. If you really believe that you have to suffer to enter the Kingdom of Heaven, then you will, simple as that.

Many Eastern sages went through the same thing because we inherently take on the path as described by our own tradition. It becomes a self-fulfilling prophecy. Anyone who has gone beyond identification with the mind into the heart of God will know the simplicity of freedom. Absolute union with God is the invitation left for us by all the mystics of all traditions.

If awakening to your True Nature is your desire, then look to those who had it fully. Look to the Teachings, I mean the direct words, of those who had the experience of awakening from the dream of separation. What is common to all of them is that it is simple, and available to everyone, and present *now*. There is no suffering mentioned, except as the thing to be transcended. There are none excluded or more worthy or able.

We live in blessed times as there are living and publicly available Self realized beings in the world. Their message is the same. The experience is One.

10. Why do I feel that God is absent from my life?

It is never the case that God is absent from someone's life. This is simply the mind throwing up a very attractive thought to keep you from being in the one place God is…Here and Now.

To even be aware of the fact that God has been absent, you must follow the mind into the past as a point of reference for that statement, you have to live in the past to keep that perspective alive. Here and now the presence of God is; and the mind is not. The simple and very humbling truth is that God has always been present in your life. You, on the other hand, have not been.

I lived my whole life never quite experiencing anything fully, and didn't even know it. My life was so full of rich experiences, but I was so busy thinking that I never actually fully experienced any of it. I wasn't there in my work, I wasn't there in my studies, I wasn't there in my relationships. The only respite from this was to turn on the television in an attempt to numb or distract myself from the ceaseless and tiring barrage of thought that I believed was me.

Although the circumstances may vary, virtually everyone I know lives their lives like this, always at least a moment away from a full experience of now. The result is that we never really experience life. We miss the richness and fullness and magic of life because we are mentally somewhere else. Every thought contains the component of time. Every thought is about the past or the future, even the ones that *appear* to be current. While we are identified with thought, experiencing the present moment is impossible. What a tragedy it is to be born and not really experience fully what it means to be alive.

The thought that God has not been present, for a spiritual seeker, is painful. The hook is the subtle desire to feel lost and alone and forsaken; in plainer words, to be special. There is a pay off for you in that, a reward for the ego, even though it is painful. It is a shock to realize that there is some kind of reward for suffering, yet it is true. Eternal Peace is here always. If there is no subtle reward for you in suffering, why do you do it?

At all costs the mind must keep you in the past, or the future. When you see this dance you can surrender the perceived pay off of separation and be present...show up for your own life and you may just discover that God was here waiting for you the whole time.

11. With so much spiritual material available these days, how does one even know where to begin?

It is true there is a mountain of spiritual material available these days, and yet little of it is of any real value if what you want is to remember what you are. Always be vigilant for what enlivens your experience now. There are a lot of things out there that feel enlivening when you read them, yet so little of it has anything to do with your experience.

It is wise to be aware of the essence of the Teaching of the great teachers who came already. They all talked about your freedom not lying off in another moment and that the realization of your True Nature is imminent, and simple.

I have never believed that after Jesus left his body he realized he had forgotten to tell everyone about spaceships and extra strands of DNA and so found some lady in Glastonbury or Sedona to speak through to tell the world the missing part of the message! It seems like everything of importance was said. The Kingdom of Heaven is within, and it is at hand. Forget about the past and stop worrying about the future. Open your awareness to the present moment and you will find it.

If you are serious about enlightenment then at some point you will have to recognize the simplicity of the dance. The most direct teachings are the simplest. You are already that which you seek.

It is necessary to see where you want to gather more and more information about the reality of consciousness. No amount of information will take you to it. In fact, it is a distraction. Any material that is of spiritual value will help you only to see that the inner journey is worth it. It can serve to leave you prepared for some of the experiences along the way, and especially to inspire you to walk the path for yourself. Seek valid guidance and know that it is simple.

Trust your journey. Every experience you have ever had has led you to this moment, and so no time has been wasted, none. It is simply a matter of remaining open and keeping freedom as your top priority.

A lot of the things I read and heard that inspired me ten years ago I can't even look at any more, but they served at the time. The things that inspire me now I was in no way ready to hear then. This is a continuum, a grand adventure that expands forever. When you know the goal however, have the courage to do what it takes. There will come a point when you have matured enough spiritually that wasting time on frivolous things, or deciding to gather more information is a delay mechanism. The experience of your true nature cannot be found in a book or on a CD, it is only by applying the teaching of moving your awareness beyond the limited mind that it can be found.

12. At what point could someone say, 'I am enlightened?'

No truly enlightened being would say that. There is no mechanism left for an individual claiming of any state. An awakened being would not be able to see themselves as special because, at the very least, they would see everyone in their universe as already free, only *believing* they are not.

For anyone who has even heard of enlightenment, there is this subtle idea that there is a destination to arrive at, and then having arrived there, there is nowhere else to go, no more to be experienced. This is not the case.

The moment you begin to recognize the quality of awareness itself, to see that it is only thought that pulls you out of the present moment, you are already moving into an enlightened state. You are shining the light of consciousness onto the shadow of ignorance. You can only be ignorant by ignoring something, and you can only end that ignorance by allowing awareness to shine upon it. It isn't anything complicated.

If a teaching becomes more about the Teacher and his or her state of consciousness than it is about the experience of the students, then something is getting out of balance. If any given moment is about someone showing off how amazing their particular experience is, then the teaching is already losing purity.

Those who are aware of their true nature need claim nothing for themselves. They may share their experience to underscore the reality of the teaching, and yet there need be no claiming of anything.

If you go to a course or a talk and it starts out with the person telling you they are enlightened, ask for your money back. If you hear people talking about whether or not someone is enlightened, don't listen. They couldn't possibly know. The mind can know nothing about freedom, and freedom cannot possibly see itself as anything special.

The truest of teachings are not rooted in "Hey, look at me and what I have," they are far more about, "Hey look at you, can't you see how magnificent you are?"

Freedom from limitation is so easy. Focusing on anything other than that is a complete waste of time.

13. How do I strike a balance between my spiritual and secular life?

Begin by realizing that there is not a split between that which you think is spiritual and that which is not. There are some adjustments in priorities maybe, like taking some time to meditate, maybe taking some time to go on retreat just to get a consistency of focus and guidance, but there are not two things here. It is not like there is the world and then there is God. There are not signs in the street saying, "Turn back now or forever leave the territory of the Absolute."

If the Source of all is literally the Source of *all*, then it is everywhere forever. It is those very divisions in the mind that lead to a seeming split. The fact is you can have all of it. A life lived with the conscious awareness of limitless peace is a life in balance. From that platform, if anything about your life needs to change, you will know.

Simply be still and let it unfold. It is wise to realize that since all of your life has always been spiritual, then you have always had, and have now, exactly what you need to be free.

Your life is your path.

CHAPTER 2

The Nature of the Self

Throughout history, in all traditions and cultures, vast amounts have been written on the true nature of the Self. This is testimony to the fact that the greatest of all human quests is the answer to the eternal question, "Who am I?"

Some of the most ancient and profound of these texts originate from India: the Upanishads, Yoga Sutras, and the Vedas. Many of these texts have been expounded upon by philosophers and scholars, most of whom had great knowledge about the texts, but little personal experience of their essence. This is one of the reasons that realizing the true Self is often seen as a difficult thing. On the contrary, realizing the true Self is actually the simplest thing in the world, it is easier than taking your next breath. It is your natural state, your most authentic being. How can it be difficult to be that which you already are? Surely it would be more difficult to be that which you are not. If it is so simple, why is it that everyone does not experience this state all the time?

When you ask someone "Who are you?" the answer is nearly always along the same lines. This is my name, I am a male (or female), I am this many years old, this is what I do for a living, I have this many children, I live in this place, etc. All of these things are *qualities* of an individual life, but the question still remains unanswered, "Who is the 'I?'" *Child of God   Child of Light*

When you look out and experience your world, who is it that is experiencing? Is it the eyeballs that see? Is it the nerve endings in the skin, the fingers and toes that experience reality? Or is it the lump of soft, pink flesh in the center of the skull that is the point where the "I" lives? Maybe "I" am simply the sum total of all these things, an accidental point of reference in a sea of sensory data.

The idea that consciousness is the artifact of electrical and chemical impulses, miraculously coordinated throughout the human nervous system is fast falling away. The human nervous system is being discovered for what it truly is, a vehicle for the Self to experience this magical multiplicity we call life. The root cause of all human pain and suffering is that we have become identified with all of the *qualities* of our existence. We believe that the "I" is the content of our lives, rather than the context.

In order to experience what you are, all that is required is to let go of what you are not. All that is required is to continually surrender every thought, feeling and action back to its Source. This need not be difficult, nor take a long time. For most of us, all that is required is a practical and efficient tool, valid guidance, and the willingness to give this development a chance.

It is irrelevant how much knowledge you have accumulated, or what you believe to be true. It is irrelevant whether or not you have lived what you might call a "good" life. Age, sex and culture are also irrelevant. When all thought, belief and judgment are surrendered, the true Self stands revealed. It is Self-evident and Self-revealing. It is absolute stillness. It is silent, aware, and intense presence. It is beyond all concepts and beliefs, crystal clear, boundless consciousness. It is beyond any thought, yet is all-intelligent. It is beyond all emotion and feeling, yet it is the ultimate bliss. It is a state of absolute wholeness; full and complete. In a world that is constantly changing, it is the One Unchanging. It is unshakeable, infinite Peace.

eternal life eternal peace of christ w/ christ

14. What is the difference between the little "s" self and the true Self?

When the little "s" self is mentioned, it is basically the ego being referred to, or the individual body/mind. This is the self that is never still and is always in search of the next thing. It is nothing more than identification with a bundle of thoughts and feelings called the mind. The sense of this self is determined by the quality and quantity of the movements in the mind. The kind of thoughts you appear to be having, the kind of feelings you appear to be having tell you who you are and how you are doing.

This is the ultimate case of mistaken identity. This self is always limited, always. Its limits are determined by beliefs, which it voluntarily gives power to. The small "s" self exists to take, even when that taking is masked by supposed service to others. It is always motivated by the perception of personal reward. Identification with this self is the root of all human pain and suffering, yet it is nothing more than a bundle of thoughts which are given the label "me."

The big "S" Self, the true Self, on the other hand, is eternally free. It is the *witness* of the thoughts and feelings that move through the mind, and yet is not affected by them. It is the Self of all beings, of all of existence. The true Self *is* existence.

I would call it the God self. The true God is the essence of who you are.

It is silent, aware, still, content, supremely un-invested, and absolutely loving. In fact, it is love. It gives constantly without investment or need for personal reward. It loves without condition or attachment. It needs nothing from the outside because it is perfect and whole and complete exactly as it is. Its qualities cannot be imitated by the mind. *I believe their is time & Investment with God, It's word, Holy Spirit to know & feel his power & direction*

yes

The realization of the true Self does not look any particular way. There is only the bliss of the Absolute. The Self is unborn and undying… it is timeless and formless. It is your true nature, and the true nature of all things. It is the silent presence of your own being and in an instant, identification can return to That. This permanent shift in perspective is what is referred to as enlightenment. To continue to focus on the mind and body as the only reality is ignorance.

15. What is the true "I?"

released to be God
dependent on or God

The true "I" is pure awareness beyond all qualities. When this awareness becomes identified with the movements of the mind, it believes that it is separate and limited, prone to harm and death. By releasing the attachment to the mind and its incessant thinking, the silent presence of your own being becomes clear. Automatically, by moving beyond identification with thought and movement, consciousness returns to its natural state.

yes

Throughout every instant of your life, through every experience, there has been one thing that has always been constant, one thing is unchanging, within all of the constant changes of life. That thing is your own silent awareness, and that is the true "I."

essence of God if cognizant

Light enters the eye and information goes to parts of the brain, but it is the "I" that sees. Vibrations move through space and make certain bones move in the ear, but it is the "I" that hears. All experience arises within your awareness. That awareness is without quality. It is still and silent. It is omnipresent and without limitation of any kind, and you are That.

16. How do I identify with the true Self?

The key to identifying with your true self is to let go of identification with the false. Anything that changes cannot be your true self. That means that your thoughts, which are constantly changing, cannot be you.

This realization is a huge relief, because until you experience it for yourself, the quality of the thoughts in your head very much determines your experience of life. Good thoughts will mean you are having a good day, bad thoughts will mean you are having a bad day. Once you see the true nature of thoughts as objective to you, they no longer have the power to influence your state of being.

Along with thoughts, your feelings are constantly changing too. The mind interprets emotion as good or bad, desired or not, and so we try to move towards, or cling on to, emotional states we like, and avoid completely those we do not. Once experienced clearly, even the movement of energy called emotion no longer has the power to influence your state of being.

Even your body is constantly changing around you. You can experience your body as objective to you. It can be witnessed in the same way that thoughts and feelings can. You *have* a body, but you are not that, and so even the changing body, once experienced clearly, no longer has the power to influence your state of being.

As you see this all for yourself, and you recognize that you are *not* your thoughts, you are *not* your feelings, and you are *not* your body, what you *are* becomes increasingly clear. You will begin to experience that you are unchanging awareness, innocent and free.

Once you have a clear experience of the silent, witnessing consciousness you can allow your attention to rest there whenever you remember. It doesn't take long for awareness to remember its original state.

In the same way that pure awareness identified with movement and forgot its true nature, so it can identify with stillness and remember. This is the path.

17. How do I know that I am moving in the right direction?

The most reliable indication that you are moving into the experience of your true Self is an experience of stillness. You could say that peace and joy are increasing and ultimately that is true, but if you relate peace and joy to a *feeling* at all, then at some point that feeling may change. It would then be easy to assume that you are moving in the wrong direction, or that you have lost the experience all together if these feelings go.

There are no external indicators that are reliable to tell that you are moving into the Self. There is really no *moving* into it. You are either experiencing it, or you are not. Stillness is the essence of the Self, and funnily enough it is the one thing the mind cannot imitate.

The mind can imitate happiness or feelings of intensity or even love, in an emotional sense. The one thing the mind cannot do is be still, because the nature of mind is movement, and movement only. No movement, no mind.

It is not that the thoughts will go away initially, but as you learn to rest more and more fully in your true nature, they cease to be a problem. The thoughts become the content in an endless sea of unmoving stillness. As you innocently rest there more and more, the belief that you are separate from that stillness dissolves quite naturally.

In all things, seek stillness. Whenever you become aware, just gently rest into yourself and allow stillness to come to you. It absolutely will. Don't even listen to your mind comment on the level of stillness it thinks you are having. Stay open and let the stillness have you.

It's amazing because if you do that, just simply rest and be still now, you will experience slightly more peace than you did a moment before, so the "reward," if you like, is instant. If you can fall in love with the simplicity of this moment, then the idea that there is somewhere else to get to, or something more you need to do, dissolves. "Growth" takes care of itself. All of that happens by grace. Your only job is to rest and be open to Presence as if it's the first time you ever did. This is innocence and it is the doorway to true peace.

18. If my true essence is pure silence, why does it seem so elusive?

It only appears that the Silence within is elusive. It is omnipresent and so can be easily discovered at any moment. The problem is only that the mind will always have an idea of what it should be looking for, and that idea is never, ever correct.

The truth is, awareness passes through infinite silence tens of thousands of times every day, as we swing from one thought to another, but we don't recognize it. Movement and sensory experience have become our only reality, and so when formlessness presents itself we discard it immediately, or pretend it never happened at all.

Almost nobody has been shown how to let go and simply experience what is there when we do. Guidance that will help you wake up is the rarest of things. Even on a spiritual path, more often than not, it is the sensory that is sought after. The ability to see lights, or heal sickness or experience trumpeting angels as a sign you have found the goal. This doesn't happen. Remembering your past lives is *not* freedom. Discovering the perfect, radiant silence of this moment *is*. The direct experience of pure awareness is not at all elusive, but the mind will constantly try to pull you from it by holding some idea about a grander, richer experience you are *supposed* to be having.

This is why guidance is so important. You cannot think your way out of your mind. You cannot self-refer your way to freedom, because everything, and I mean everything the mind believes about what freedom is like, is wrong. The mind cannot know about freedom because its very nature is limitation. Having someone who has gone beyond the mind to help you do the same allows you the space to return to innocence, to no longer need to figure it out for yourself.

The whole thing is incredibly easy. When you are ready to go beyond the need for sensory entertainment, there is a clear and direct path home. Nothing about you ever needs to be fixed to get there. The only thing you need to remember is how to let go.

19. Is the true Self separate from Creation?

Reverse the order of your question. *Nothing* is separate from the true self. All things are rooted in the same source, and this source is your true self. Having said that, the appearance of creation has no influence whatsoever on the true self. It remains untouched by all apparent movement and change. It is the unchanging, eternal source of all experience. It is the pure, aware field from which everything spontaneously appears, and *to* which everything returns.

As awareness of your true nature unfolds, the inherent unity of all things becomes clear. Everything is perceived as radiant, with its own divine perfection. Like reflections dancing on the surface of a still pond, all form is seen as an exquisite reflection on the endless ocean of divinity. It becomes crystal clear that all apparent diversity and difference is rooted in the same thing, and indeed is not separate from it.

The experience of creation is simply the perfect unfolding of divinity expressing itself, including *you*, by the way. Evolution is simply the continuous unfolding of creation. There really is no separation between anything, only the appearance of it.

It is your birthright to experience this, that there have never been two things. To live your life with a constant experience of the perfect unfolding of divinity is your natural state. No fear, no doubt, no guilt or shame, no sense of lack or unworthiness; this is the way of true human experience. Anything other is a *learned* reality, and as such, it can be *un*-learned. This is the good news!

20. I have heard the Self described as a void. What is the void?

It is a misinterpretation. To look for the void is a trap, because by searching for the "void," most people are searching for emptiness. All descriptions of the supreme state, which have come from those having the experience, have alluded to it being beyond qualities, and yet there is nothing empty about it.

When Buddha used the term "Nirvana," he was referring to that which is beyond all description. The inner, silent presence is beyond all limited references to qualities, and yet, it is infinitely full at the same time. Buddha said to hold every experience with an open hand, and this is powerful advice. It was a warning, neither to grasp for some kind of experience, nor to push anything away. It is simply to rest and be aware without investment. From that space, the awareness can be moved inward to ever-deeper levels, at the same time as surrendering all boundaries to the presence of God.

Existence is absolute. There is no possibility of a non-existent state. God has no opposite. It is an uncaused, eternal field of silent awareness and infinite potential, within which *all* things appear.

It is possible for the mind to hold the *thought* of nothingness. Lifetime after lifetime it will be drawn back to transcend that most subtle of limitations. In one incredible moment, the experience of emptiness can be surrendered, and awareness is absorbed forever into the All-ness of God.

21. What is the soul?

What most people refer to as the soul is actually the mind. It is the subtlest level of the mind still believing it is separate and evolving back to one-ness with God, forever getting a little closer, a little closer, which in truth is delaying freedom.

guilt is a tool of Satan or "other" not of God.

The soul, in this context, is the part of the mind that still carries enough guilt about the idea of separating from God that it will seemingly move on and on, from lifetime to lifetime, endlessly seeking healing and the learning of lessons, forever just a breath away from home. The belief that we need to atone for our sins, that we need to suffer just enough to catch the attention and compassion of the Divine is the nastiest belief in the collective consciousness of humanity. It is a lie.

I believe we get free of any bondage when we ask God for forgiveness.

In this amazing dream world, we can play it out any way we like. The belief that we need to be improved to be worthy of love, the belief

that there are things about us that need to be healed through the
learning of lessons, is a self-perpetuating experience. As you believe,
so it is. At some point, there comes the recognition that the love of
God is not dependant upon anything other than the fact that you
exist, and that you are worthy of it *now*. There is no judgment from
the Divine that some are more worthy than others, or that some are
less worthy. All judgment is from the limited, individual mind.

Yes some Christians don't feel worthy.

If you can embrace this, then comes the revelation of the soul as it truly
is. In consciousness, all experience is recorded forever. All choices
and the resulting consequences are known eternally. Consciousness is
the repository of the playing out of infinite potential. This "database"
of living experience is the lifeblood of the true soul. There is an
aspect of the infinite field of consciousness that is aware. It is the one
witness of all minds, the "I" of all of creation, the Self and essence
of all things. It is the true "experiencer." There is one soul, and it is
God's. It is not different from God itself, and neither are you. *yes ☺*

22. What is the most effective approach to union with God?

A sincere approach is the most effective. It is one thing to be enlivened
by the concept of eternal peace, but quite another to go for it and
discover this most glorious of states for yourself. The journey into
the heart of God requires one to take the awareness inward, beyond
the mind, and to surrender the attachment to limitation. In order to
discover the Real, it is necessary only to recognize the false, and let
it go. This is not difficult, but it does require you to want to wake
up, to desire freedom above all else.

Meditation, true meditation is invaluable for this. It allows you the
space to see the mind for what it is and to go beyond. As you do
this, the eternally available presence of the true Self becomes clear

as the witness. Beyond the witness is the unconditioned All-ness of pure consciousness.

Union with God is the revelation of this state as the Self. It is the recognition that the presence, the mind, the body and the world have always only ever been one thing without separation. This experience cannot be forced, and is far beyond mentally claiming the state as your own. By opening yourself to your own presence now, this moment becomes so fulfilling in and of itself, that the desire to be somewhere or something else dissolves. The final steps are then open to grace.

There is a concept that it is somehow necessary to kill the ego or stop the mind in order to be free, but in truth it is really only about ending your identification with those things, changing your relationship to them.

The most effective approach to union with God will always be the most simple. You have probably heard a million times, "You are already that which you seek." But this does little of much value when all you know of yourself is a bunch of thoughts that sound just like you. Simplicity is everything. The path of awakening is learning to distinguish what you are from what you are not. It is discovering the simple, silent presence that exists beyond the mind and learning to rest there. When you are ripe, reality shines forth in its full glory.

If you are in this presence You are of love of light you are awake as you say.

Unfortunately, as one begins to tread the path to awakening, it is easy to slowly make peace less than the first priority. If freedom and eternal peace is what you desire, it must be the thing you thirst for more than anything else, the one thing that motivates your entire life. This level of commitment and desire are necessary to avoid being sucked back in to the old familiar habits of limitation. The journey is not difficult, but it does require 100 percent commitment.

Commitment to love God and be/follow His will 100% not to be driven by hatred, guilt, condemnation, lack.
Psalm 23 : The Lord is my shepherd I lack nothing.

The flip side of this is that if your commitment to attaining the goal is absolute, the universe will rush to support you in that. Everything will line up to bring you to <u>Self-realization</u> in the shortest possible time. <u>It is a joint venture between you</u> and God, but you must always be willing to take the first step, and remain <u>committed</u> to what it is you say you want. This is complete alignment of thought, word and deed. Half-hearted commitment brings half-hearted results…this is natural law.

Committed to God's will & path for you.

CHAPTER 3

Transcending Limitation

One of the most common themes of personal and spiritual development is the focus on destroying or conquering the ego in order to discover the Divine. The ego is sometimes seen as the adversary, wily and cunning in its own right, trying desperately to delay or prevent your freedom.

The truth is much less dramatic. What is called "ego" is nothing more than thoughts, thoughts that we have become identified with. Identification with these thoughts brings the appearance of a limited, separate self. When this is the case, our very sense of self is determined by the quality and quantity of our thoughts and feelings.

What we put our attention on grows. Ego has no independent existence, and so to put energy into destroying it merely gives it artificial life. To go to battle with it merely gives reality to something that, in and of itself, is not real.

There are places in these dialogues where the ego or separate self is talked about as if it actually exists. This is a convenience of language, a way to build a bridge between that which the student knows and that which they do not, or at least, that which they do not yet remember.

We all know very well what it feels like to be constantly driven by thought. We know what it is like to live in fear or to feel like there are things about us that are unlovable or limited. What most people do *not* know however, is what it is like to live without these limiting beliefs, to live free of the movements of the mind with a conscious experience of the silent presence which lies beyond.

Undoing the attachment to the mind allows consciousness to once again rest in its true nature. The Ishayas have always taught that it is not necessary to "kill" the ego, only to stop identifying with it. The techniques of Ascension have this as their only purpose, to rise beyond the identification with the limited mind into a direct experience of the perfect peace within.

23. What is duality?

You should know full well what duality is. Have you ever experienced conflict? How about suffering? Fear? Living a dual existence brings all of these states about. Duality is the perception of two things, and it is the root of all human suffering.

If you live from this state, there is always the possibility of being hurt. There is always the possibility of lack and fear, because there seem to be forces external to you that are a constant threat. It is all mind created and yet seems so real when it is the only experience of life one has.

Virtually everyone who has ever lived has only experienced this state. It is the state where, when something happens to me, it must be *your* fault. There is constant blame and defense. I will reinforce my position, and fight to the death if it is threatened.

It is a life of constant judgment. I am doing the right thing, and you are not. You are less, or sometimes more, worthy than me. It divides the world up into imaginary boxes, and plants flags in them. It is the, "My God's better than your God, and he's gonna kick your God's ass!" mentality.

No matter how it manifests, the state of duality is driven by fear.

There is another perspective that could be called unity. It is the recognition that all things are of one source. When you know yourself *as* that source, the possibility of fear is gone, because what could exist outside of you to fear? In the experience that you are intrinsically linked to an endless field of love, there is no sense of lack or shame possible. You are whole and complete, worthy of love and wholeness simply because you exist. There is no sense that you could fail because nothing is expected of you, other than to be free.

There is no judgment because all things are seen to be unfolding perfectly, all people are always doing the best that they can. Infinite love is seen as the only reality, all else is recognized as illusion. To transcend dualistic perception is the invitation of your life. It is, in fact, your purpose.

24. How does one transcend duality?

The only way to transcend duality is to transcend the mind. Not by killing it or beating it into submission, but simply by seeing it for what it is, and going beyond. In seeing the false as false, you will find Truth.

The mind exists in duality; this is its nature. When you believe the content of the mind to be you, then duality becomes your experience. Said another way, you have simply identified with the perception of movement, which is fleeting and transient, and forgotten your true nature as eternal, radiant consciousness. Then begins the struggle away from pain and toward pleasure and you are trapped, like a rat in a box. To get out of it, you have to go beyond the mind. This is surprisingly easy.

Mind sees this and that, right and wrong, down and up, in and out, me and you; always opposites. Awareness simply sees without judgment, without commentary. Begin by watching your mind. Once you begin to see that thought can be there, like an object, you have already experienced a shift in consciousness. That which is aware of thought cannot be the thought itself.

The same thing applies to feelings. At any moment you could tell me how you are feeling. Again, you can describe the emotional state only because you are able to witness it objectively, at least to some degree. The same thing applies here too; that which is *aware* of the feeling cannot be the feeling itself.

Take this a step further, and you can see and experience your body. You can observe it, and see that it is actually objective to you. If you were to lose a finger or an arm, it would not diminish *you*. You may believe that it would, but this is because there is still the belief that you *are* you body, rather than you *have* a body.

There are many cases of those who have lost a limb, and can actually experience phantom sensations where the limb used to be! A finger or an arm does not have the capability to experience itself. The senses collect data from the environment, but it is consciousness that interprets this, and creates a reality.

These are usually sequential leaps in awareness, and it begins with cultivating the ability to watch thoughts. Simply by beginning to see the movements of the mind as separate from you, the experience of the inner silence begins to open. The more familiar one becomes with that silence, the appearance of movement can be surrendered and let go of.

After the surface thoughts are surrendered, the commentating voices beneath become apparent and can be surrendered to the Silence also. The commentator is the little voice in the head that sounds like you, telling you how well you are doing, how you are progressing, how you are failing, and coaching you along in your life. Eyes open and eyes closed, once the commentator is surrendered, any doubt that you are anything other than unconditioned awareness evaporates. What is left is only silence. What is left is only God. No separation, no duality.

This journey is made infinitely easier with a valid and effective tool for taking the awareness inward, and the guidance of those who understand how to go beyond the subtleties of the mind.

25. How do I get rid of my ego?

There is no need to get rid of or kill your ego. In fact, this as a direct goal is impossible. It is important for you to hear this. By going about spiritual growth in this way you are fighting something that was never real in the first place. You are going to battle with something that does not exist, so you unnecessarily delay your freedom.

It is not the perception of the ego that is the problem; it is your *identification* with it. This beast named the ego is nothing more than a bunch of thoughts whose voices sound disturbingly like you. All that is required is to become identified with what is *aware* of these thoughts.

If you were sitting in your living room watching TV and your pet dog walked in, you wouldn't all of a sudden forget who you are. You would simply notice her walk in, and then go back to your bowl of popcorn.

With some guidance and a valid teaching you can cultivate this same relationship with what you call your ego. You have a pet called Gary, that's all. Sometimes he's there, sometimes he isn't. At no time does the presence or absence of Gary need to affect your experience. Enjoy it, but in the midst of every experience, learn to rest in your true Self, which is devoid of qualities, and is bliss itself.

Everything exists within a space. If you read a book, you can only see the words because there is a blank page for them to appear upon. If you look at a painting, you can only see it because there is a blank canvas for it to appear upon. "Gary" is only discernable because there is an infinitely bigger space of "no Gary" for it to appear within. Seek that space and freedom is swift.

It is only the identification with, and investment in Gary that keeps you locked in it. This includes the desire to have Gary gone or to get rid of Gary. It is all about space, about context.

You have the ability to put your attention on the context of any experience, that is the space within which it appears. Out of habit you are identified with content, the form, the movement. Virtually all of humanity has this case of mistaken identity. We are only taught to see form, and consequently forget the formless.

When I was a child, my family moved to Australia from England. It is a very different climate. England is famous for its cloud cover, and

Australia is famous for the opposite. I would hear people constantly remarking on the nice weather. "What a beautiful day," they would say, "There isn't a cloud in the sky."

It is a very common way to say it, but it shows that as a rule, we do not allow ourselves to experience that which is beyond qualities. Even the enormous expanse of the sky is described in terms of the presence or absence of clouds.

This is even truer of our experience of ourselves. We are constantly experiencing ourselves in relation to the quantity and especially quality, of our thoughts and feelings. The transient and often volatile movement of thought is the barometer of humanity's sense of self.

Learn to discover and rest in the unmoving, formless context of every experience, the space within which it appears. Allow the mind to be as it will and go beyond it into the silent, witnessing presence. Learn to find that, rest there and freedom is swift and easy.

26. How does one go beyond suffering?

The first step is to believe that it is possible. Without the belief that it is possible, one would not even begin the journey. In order to transcend suffering, it is necessary to find the source of all suffering and duality; and that is something that only exists within you.

With a little investigation, it can be seen that suffering and duality are caused primarily by your attachment to your mind and the things that you believe to be true. Once you begin to see this for yourself, then you can rise beyond it.

Many pull back from the experience of true peace because it is so unfamiliar to us. We will refuse to give up the separation, which although painful, is at least familiar. The mind will justify its positions by telling you that suffering is *not* all about you, it is really about other peoples' pain. It is not. It is always about you and by this realization alone can you be free. If you want to be free of suffering and rest again in the heart of God, you need to investigate your own relationship with your mind.

For most people, the thoughts and judgments that flow through the mind very much sound like "me." The voices in our head have *our* voice. What these voices say about us, and our relationship to the world is then seen as truth. Because of the subtle beliefs we have cultivated, the mind divides the world, and ourselves, into good and bad.

As awareness is allowed to expand and the mind becomes objectively witnessed, these thoughts can be seen as just movement. The sense of self is clearly experienced as bigger than thoughts. This is what expanding awareness means. It is all about expanding context.

Through the forgetting of our true nature, we have become identified with content, with movement, with "stuff." This "stuff" has the seeming ability to determine our experience of the world and ourselves. Expansion of consciousness is about making the shift from content to *context*.

It becomes evident that the content exists always within a bigger space, and that space is your own awareness. The more solid this realization becomes, the less power the "stuff" has over your state of being. Once content is surrendered to context completely, duality is over, judgment is over, suffering is over and what remains is eternally free.

27. How do I find out where I am holding onto my limitations?

Luckily, this is not really necessary. You will see them as you need to, and from there, surrendering them to God is the path. It is not necessary, however, to discover what all of your limitations are, because that keeps the focus on what you are leaving behind, rather than what you are moving towards. One of those perspectives is challenging and hard; the other is a joyful exploration of continuously expanding freedom.

If you *do* find yourself stuck on something, it can get tricky if you want to find the actual limitation that is causing it. Most of your positions are linked in some way, and so it can appear complicated. Leave all that to therapy.

Ultimately, you are stuck because your ego is getting a reward out of holding on to the position. "I'll prove them wrong," "I'll prove I'm right," "I'll show them all," "I know best what is good for you," "I'll never get it so it's better not to even begin." *reward*

Uhmmn? True or Not peace

We continue to run the negative program because there is some self-righteous reward in it. We remain angry with our neighbor because it reminds us we are right. Get over it. You know someone, or may even be someone, who has lived a long time holding a grudge or grievance against someone else. This puts enormous stress on the nervous system and holds the position in place.

It's almost as if we try to punish the other person by putting ourselves through stress! "I'm going to get back at you by raising my blood pressure and my heart rate and moving myself towards an early grave." It's crazy when you see it like that. The best revenge is to be free!

If you want to be free you have to surrender the need to be right. You cannot be right *and* free in the same moment. Trust me, I tried!

So, see what your ego is getting out of your positions and let *that* go. It is far easier than trying to identify all of the positions themselves.

28. What are the greatest blocks to awakening?

There is no external block to awakening; no hidden traps set to ensnare the spiritual seeker. There is only the belief that your internal positions and judgments are valid. The entirety of ignorance is based in identification with thought, and the entirety of awakening is surrendering those thoughts to the infinite freedom of the present.

Believing that it is not possible to be free is a block to the experience, until you are willing to let it go and see what happens. Not believing you are worthy of love is a block, until you are willing to let it go and see what happens. It is merely the willingness to let go now and see what happens that brings about the magical transformation of consciousness that is called waking up.

As one evolves, the nature of the positions preventing further growth changes. "I'm finally free." "I'm enlightened now." "I'm one with everything." These kinds of thoughts are still just thoughts, and as such, need to be surrendered also.

Then there are the feelings associated with higher states of consciousness. Bliss, for example, or love. It's not that these are bad experiences by any means, but they are something that can be grasped as some kind of indicator of progress, thereby preventing further surrender to the infinite. These too, must be surrendered, not to get rid of them, or push them away, but so that you are holding nothing and surrendering all experiences back to their source. Beyond any experience there is always a greater state, and the key to the door is surrender.

There are not an infinite number of things keeping you from freedom; there is really only one. Identification with movement is it. Little by little, or all at once, the movement can be surrendered to the experience of perfect stillness and silence. In that experience truth is revealed, wholeness is revealed, love is revealed and freedom is revealed.

Don't get hooked up in making this more complicated than it is. Freedom is endlessly simple and achievable by all.

29. How will I function in the world if I let go of my mind?

This is actually a very common question, and is simply born from the fear of the unknown. You actually know the experience very well, but have simply forgotten. You are remembering how to function differently, yet you will function. Your mind will still be there when you need to use it, but your relationship to it will be changed forever.

While you have a body you will have a mind, but it will no longer run your life. It will no longer limit your experience by keeping you locked in fear and self-limiting patterns. Even the way you experience the mind itself will change. Instead of a constant stream of linear thought, you begin to interact with the world through a kind of refined intuition. Life becomes a sequence of silent knowingness from within, wordless and yet intimate.

Any time you have excelled, you have functioned like this. In fact the greatest of all human achievements have always come from a silent knowingness when the mind is surrendered for a moment.

Archimedes was searching for a way to measure the mass of gold in the king's crown. The sticking point was that the king forbade him to damage or destroy the crown in any way. He couldn't figure it out. He tried and tried and couldn't get it. Eventually he said, "Screw it, I'm going for a bath." and in a moment of letting go of trying to figure it out mentally, resting in that bath, he discovered displacement, a brilliant way to calculate mass.

Sir Isaac Newton did the same thing. He was pondering how things stick to the Earth, but he just couldn't get it. He took a break to drink some tea with a friend under some apple trees and "Bam!" Literally. An apple fell on his head and the law of gravity was officially discovered.

All artists, poets, writers, and musicians know this experience. The greatest artistic expression comes when we are out of the way. The greatest works come spontaneously and intuitively from within.

This is not *only* true for artists. The most fulfilling experiences of anyone's life happen in the same way. In the most wonderful moments of anyone's life, the fulfillment always arises spontaneously from within, in a moment of getting out of your own way. These moments need not be caused by anything physically spectacular, but something catches our attention, the mind is surrendered, and we are immersed in the beauty of the present moment.

The most effective solutions to life's challenges seem to come from out of nowhere. This can only happen when we let go of the surface of the mind for a moment, and a moment is all it takes.

For most people, however, the experience of silent intuition is spontaneous and not recognized consciously. As a result, after the experience has passed, the attention is then directed back into the mind to try and find the best way to apply what has intuitively presented itself.

Intuitive knowingness happens in all kinds of mundane situations as well. We have all had experiences where we have lost something. We lose our car keys and search frantically for them. We look over and over in all the places that we know we left them, but to no avail. So many times, when we just give up the search, all of a sudden, in the eye of the mind, the picture of exactly where the keys are pops into our awareness. Lo and behold, we look in that spot and there they are. So many times and in so many ways this happens.

The best thing you can do is to discover for yourself the still, silent place within, and learn to rest there. It will fill you up automatically and life will become increasingly fluid. You may find, as everyone I know who has discovered the silence within has found, that every area of life becomes more effective, enjoyable and easy.

Your natural state is one of awe and wonder, empty of linear thought. It is a continuous stream of innocence and pure experience, alive and radiant. It is the source of all genius, the source of all beauty, the source of all love, and it is only obscured by clinging to the surface of the mind.

30. I am a loner and don't want to connect with anyone else.

Maybe that is how it appears to you, but it is not true. Somewhere inside you is an immense desire to connect and give to the rest of humanity, but it is obscured by some pattern that you have picked up that says you don't deserve that connection, or that you will ultimately end up being hurt in some way.

It is one thing not to *need* anyone else for your sense of self-worth, but it is another thing entirely to believe that you don't want any kind of connection at all, that the rest of humanity can just get on with it.

The thing about the journey of awakening is that it is not possible to do it on your own. That's a tough realization for some people, but it is true. The mind would love to be able to do everything on it's own, to be totally self-referring, but this is separation. You cannot think your way to freedom.

If you really want to wake up, then you need the guidance of someone who can help you, someone who has transcended the mind and who knows the subtleties that can pop up along the way. You need to be willing to surrender to something other than the thoughts in your head.

It is also beyond valuable to have people around you who want the same thing. That may not be in physical proximity, but to have access to those who can keep you motivated and focused in your desire to be free.

As you step, little by little, outside of the comfort zone of isolation, you will begin to see that you cannot walk the path by yourself. Not only that, but even if you could, you wouldn't want to. Sharing the journey is simply too good. Connecting with others also helps you to see that there is always more.

Once you have an inner experience of true love, the way to expand that experience is to give it away. This is natural actually. Once you have gone beyond your own suffering, automatically there comes the desire to alleviate the suffering of everyone else. As union dawns, everyone is seen as a part of you, not as separate beings. Those beings are parts of you that do not yet love themselves fully. How could you leave a part of yourself to suffer?

The truth of it is, you are not completely free until all of humanity is free. Once you learn to love yourself, then you will do whatever you can to have everyone love themselves too. This is compassion; this is true healing. Once you wake up, this is the purpose of your life.

31. I have a strong desire to know God, but I am afraid of losing control.

The root of this experience is a split desire. It may be unconscious, but it is a split desire nonetheless. You have a strong desire to know God, but as the experience inches closer, the part of your mind that actually still wants to remain in separation goes into fear. You want to be one with God, and yet at some level the "little you" still wants to remain in control.

Simply rest in the presence of your own being and observe these thoughts as they arise. As you observe and rest more, you will see for yourself that you actually *never* had control; it was just a clever ruse of the mind. The very idea that the small part of us ever had control over anything becomes very funny indeed.

If you take an honest look at your life, then it becomes obvious. There was always something greater in control, but through ignorance and forgetfulness, you just couldn't see that. Once you do begin to recognize this, however, surrender gets easier.

The whole illusion of fear, especially fear of absolute surrender, becomes quite comical. It can feel scary I know, but as you discover and become intimate with your true nature, the purity of that experience, the intense love of that presence eliminates any fear that the mind will throw at you. You will directly experience the love of God, and in this love, all fear dissolves.

The mind fears its own annihilation in the silence, and rightfully so because it cannot exist there. As you move closer to the silence in its fullness, the mind throws up thoughts and fears about non-existence. Non-existence is impossible. The silence of your true nature *is existence itself*, beginning-less and endless. Who, or rather *what*, you really are cannot be lost. Your true being is eternal. As such, it cannot be threatened. Anything that can be lost was, in reality, never real in the first place.

Try shifting your perspective a little too. Rather than *losing* yourself, you are on a journey of discovering *more* of yourself forever. The beauty of this teaching is that you can discover what lies beyond the mind really quickly and easily. If you can make your journey about where you are heading rather than what you seem to be leaving behind, it is a lot more simple and enjoyable!

You are neither the mind nor the body. You are much, much more than that. Simply continue to give yourself to peace and all else will be revealed. As is said so beautifully in *A Course in Miracles*, "Nothing real can be threatened, nothing unreal exists; herein lies the Peace of God."

32. Who am I without my thoughts? Are they not the means by which I create my reality?

This is one of the best questions you could ask. Real spiritual evolution begins when you decide to find out. The sense of a limited self, a separate self, is quite literally the product of a thought. Actually, it's not the thought that creates it, but believing yourself to be the *thinker* of the thought.

Every thought has two elements in common, regardless of the content. Every thought involves time, thereby taking your attention away from now, and every thought has an element of 'me,' thereby instantly creating the illusion of an individual identity.

While you are identified with thought, you become separate and subject to the passage of time, rather than infinite being-ness. In the sense that you believe yourself to be limited and separate, caught in a world that presents constant danger and prone to suffering and death, yes, they are the means by which you create your reality.

As you begin to watch your thoughts, to be aware of them like they are somebody else's, you can begin to discover the presence of what is called the witness. It is not subject to the quality, or even the perception, of movement. It is perfectly still, and it is the real you.

So, discover who you are without your thoughts. Discover who you are without the belief that the thoughts are yours to begin with. This is the magical doorway to a whole new discovery of self, and the key to liberation.

33. When I identify with thoughts like, "I'm fat," "I'm skinny," "I'm intelligent," "I can," "I can't," am I moving away from freedom?

Actually, in the moment you believe those thoughts, you are not moving away from the experience of freedom, you have completely left it. At any moment you take a thought seriously, you have left the infinite silent presence, and gone into the limited space of the mind. Identification with any thought is limited.

If you knew you only had five minutes left to live, and an angel came to you and said, "You have five more minutes on this planet left, so use them wisely." Would you care if you were fat or thin, male or female, intelligent or not? Would you remain angry with a family member for some trivial comment or action? Probably not.

Priorities have a way of changing in the face of death, and I would advise you to live every moment like that...like you only have five minutes left. Don't waste a moment on whether you are ready or not ready to let go, you just let go.

To focus on things that are not important is waste of your conscious energy. Life is too short to hold on to positions and judgments about yourself, or anyone else for that matter.

You said something very important that I want to bring to your attention, "When I identify with the thoughts…" The thoughts themselves do not have the power to pull you away from freedom, but when you believe them and own them rather than just allowing them to come and go, you close the door on your peace instantly.

You can still change and improve anything you want, but the changes are lasting if they are made from a space of not seeing anything wrong.

When you simply watch the thoughts and allow them to go, you can experience the presence that exists beyond the mind. What is left is complete and unconditional acceptance, an endless and universal love. In that space, all judgment ends.

It is okay that these thoughts still seem to have power over you, but the truth is if you just let them be and follow the guidance you are given here, you can totally let go of these thoughts.

34. I already feel like a very positive person. Most of my thoughts aren't negative and chaotic. Does this mean I'm free?

This can be as much of a trap as pain and suffering. Just because you have thoughts that are pleasant doesn't mean that they are necessarily expansive to your state of awareness. They are not going to set you free.

It is indeed a stage of progress to have "good" thoughts. When thoughts are pleasant however, it can be even more difficult to want to transcend the mind completely. To realize the Kingdom of Heaven, you must transcend the mind, no matter how pleasant its content. This does not mean you have to give up the good things that life has brought you. It simply means it is necessary to give up the *attachment* to them.

Here in the world you can think you have the most amazing life, the nicest thoughts, and the best stuff. In truth, it is all only *relatively* good. Your good thoughts are only good in relation to bad thoughts.

Your mind cannot even begin to imagine the bliss of the Absolute, and herein lays the problem. It's a tough nut to want to swallow when you realize that all the good things in your life are only *relatively* good, and there is something much, much greater, closer than your next breath.

No matter how happy you have made your mind, or how physically comfortable you have made your life; of what value is it when this life is over? The individual ego has had a wonderful time here on Earth, but you still don't know who you are.

The benefits of surrendering everything to God, is that not only will you discover your immortality, you open yourself to all the good stuff in your life getting better. Surrender allows you to empty yourself and to be open to the possibility that there is more. In every sense, whether it is physically, mentally or spiritually, there is always more.

If you can get to a place where you are willing to see what it is like to surrender even the good thoughts, then you are ready to be free. I am not saying it is bad to have a life that is pleasant and fun; in fact I would wish you that. I am simply saying that no matter how good your life is, if you are not aware of your true nature, then it is limited.

35. Is there a difference between purification and transcendence?

Purification means to be in a state of preparation for something. Transcendence is to let it go. That's not to say that purification may not happen, but transcendence happens when you realize that some boundary, which before seemed like an absolute truth, no longer serves you and you let it go, you surrender it back to God.

Transcendence is immediate. The belief that you need purification can be a ploy to delay your peace. Transcendence can only happen now. Purification as a goal is always going to be preparation for some future state. Peace only exists now. Freedom only exists now, and nothing about you needs to be fixed in order to experience it.

In my experience, purification has almost always been as a result of transcendence. There have been times in my life where I have had major realizations that have lead to a permanent expansion of awareness. As a result, certain habits or behaviors have been abandoned.

I know there are many schools of thought that say first purify yourself and then you will be ready to be free, but in my experience, and the experience of the most conscious people I know, it is quite the opposite. It is not even necessary that all physical impurities will be purified, even after awakening. This may or may not happen, but it is realizing the presence of God that must be first.

I know many people who have purified many areas of their lives, and while they are happier in themselves, and it has of course been a good thing, they are no closer to waking up. In fact, the very path of purification has lead to the creation of a whole new set of limiting beliefs. Many of them have cultivated the belief that one day, when they are pure enough, they will experience freedom. It is always, always the mind that says you are not worthy of freedom now. There is something else you need to do, something else you need to fix. It is the ultimate fallacy and a vicious lie.

In the mind's perception of separation there is an automatic reaction of guilt. We don't know how we ended up here, leaving the presence of God, but surely when God finds out She will be furious! There begins the endless journey of lifetimes upon lifetimes hiding from the inevitable punishment for leaving Heaven, trying to atone for our sins.

As you begin to discover the presence of God as a direct experience, you will discover the unconditional love of that presence. There becomes your direct experience that there is no judgment from the Divine. In that, the mind's self-judgment dissolves and the ultimate realization dawns...not only do you completely deserve to return home, in reality, you never left.

Nothing about you needs to be fixed to move closer to your true nature. You are now, and forever, free. All bondage, all separation, all death are dreams merely, and it is a dream that you can, and must, awaken from. If you want absolute freedom, find God first and let purification happen as it will.

Most spiritual seekers do not want to hear something like that. In fact, there are whole teachings based around creating the most pleasant life you can. This is relative freedom, which is actually not freedom at all.

This is waking up *within* the dream, which is fine, but you are being offered the opportunity to awaken FROM it.

36. I wish I had heard about this when I was younger. Do all my years of programming and habits make this harder for me? Am I too old?

That really depends on you. How strong is your desire to wake up? The only difference between you and anyone younger is that your lifelong habits of limitation may feel more familiar. This can also work in your favor. When you know your mind so intimately, then it becomes obvious that going beyond it is the only way to lasting peace. Whether you are 7, 27 or 70, the only thing holding you back is a thought. It is no harder or easier for anyone to let go.

I have met plenty of young people for whom the desire to wake up is not even attractive, even if they have quite painful lives. Most of the people I have known are quite happy with their unsatisfying and unfulfilling life. The desire to seek the purpose of it all has not even been kindled. This is not rare in the young, as life is very much an outward experience.

As one gets older however, there is a natural movement towards seeking a deeper understanding of existence. You have lived a full life, and then what? What is the point? If you really want to discover the answers to these things for yourself, then age is no barrier.

CHAPTER 4

The Evolution
of Consciousness

All of the experiences that can be shared in relation to awakening are symptoms of what is commonly called spiritual evolution. This is the appearance of awareness growing from ignorance and absorption in the individual self, to identification with the silent, self-evident all-ness of Source.

While it is the experience that consciousness evolves to experience more and more of its own True Nature, the truth is that awareness is full and complete and whole always. The perception of consciousness expanding is actually fuelled by the surrendering of limited attachments and ideas. As the small ego self is surrendered, a more glorious reality dawns. It is akin to the sun coming into view as the clouds part and dissolve in its light and warmth. The sun is there always but can be seemingly obscured from view by the clouds.

The revelation of light is always through the dissolution of that which obscures it. The light itself is unchanging and eternal.

As one embarks on the greatest of all journeys into the heart of God, many kinds of experiences begin to dawn, some of which can serve to propel growth further, some of which without adequate guidance, can serve to limit and delay freedom from suffering.

The habit of the mind is to seek the sensory. As consciousness begins to open to its true nature, the senses become heightened too. Feelings of love or joy, experiences of colors and lights, manifestation of latent powers of attention can all come into awareness. Without guidance, these things can be seen as indicators of progress, and actually be sought as the goal. This is far from true.

The one thing the mind cannot seek is silence, and it is in this silence that the revelation of true divinity occurs. Rare is the student who is ready to surrender all sensory experience to God.

Throughout history, those who have walked the path before have left teachings to share their experiences and to help others to freedom. Some of those teachings and experiences are incredibly direct and swift. Some, due primarily to lack of guidance, are caught in the mire of sensory experience and spiritually noble limitation.

Having the opportunity to share the experiences you have with those who have gone through them too is invaluable. Answers to questions serve to alleviate doubt.

It is wise to be aware of declaring to yourself, "Now I get it!" or "Now I see how it is…" because consciousness evolves forever. It is easy to make a line in the sand of your conscious evolution and not step across into a greater existence.

 As the subtler levels of the mind begin to experience a more divine reality, it can become clear that you are a part of the whole, and vice-versa. Through continual surrender of limitation, reality becomes clearer. You are not a little ray of the Divine; you are not a co-creator with God. The real you *is* the fullness of the Divine; the real you *is* God...all of it.

The truest essence of the Teaching is always transmitted silently and constantly through the presence of an awakened Teacher. Every moment spent in such a presence immeasurably propels the experience of the committed student toward the full realization of his or her own divinity.

37. Can you talk about the different stages or levels of consciousness?

Ultimately it could be said that there are no levels of consciousness. The presence of God is omnipresent. It is an infinite ocean of pure consciousness within which everything appears. It does not have a shallow end.

What happens as one begins to move into that experience is that growth seems to unfold gradually as positions, beliefs and judgments are surrendered. It is not so much that consciousness *increases* in stages, as it is that ignorance *decreases* in stages.

The average person in the world is completely oblivious to the still, silent presence within them. They are so addicted to the experience of movement and chatter that inner silence is almost never entertained as a possibility, let alone a desirable one.

Through a valid practice of taking the mind inward and with adequate guidance, one will begin to see that just beyond the surface of the mind is a direct experience of this silence. As one gives more attention to it, it seems to grow. It begins to take up increasing amounts of attention until it becomes a virtually seamless presence.

For most, this presence is first discovered during meditation with the eyes closed. In many teachings this is the goal, to be able to glimpse the stillness during meditation. The Ishayas have always held that this is only the beginning. It is not only possible for this presence to be the inner experience with the eyes closed, it is also possible, and simple, to have it as an ongoing experience as you go about your daily life. It is absolutely possible to live your life with a constant awareness of infinite silence. This may seem incredible to many, but not only is it possible, again it is only the beginning.

All of us have always lived in a world that is colored by our inner state. We have always seen the world through the filters of our own judgments and beliefs. As belief clears to reveal the divine presence within, the world we live in begins to reflect this new inner state of purity. All is seen as divine, all is seen as bathed in the presence of God.

This state is characterized by a transcendental love. All things shine forth in their divine beauty. Yet the natural habit to follow this beauty outward can literally halt growth of consciousness at this point. The key to being able to move through higher states of consciousness to unite completely with God is surrender. It is necessary to be as willing to surrender the beauty, as it is to surrender the pain, to give all experiences back to their Source.

Many spiritual traditions will tell you that this most exalted of states is not possible for the average human to experience, especially not in this lifetime. Again, the Ishayas have not only known it is possible, but that there is even more than this.

The willingness to surrender even the divine beauty and love of this level of awareness is necessary to unite fully with God. At this point, there is the direct recognition of the Divine within and without at the same time, and yet there is a subtle demarcation between the two things. There is an almost imperceptible "me."

Having a tool and guidance that facilitates the surrender of this limited "me" to the Absolute is critical to reach the goal of human life. As this belief in a separate "me" experiencing everything dissolves, reality shines forth in its full splendor. There is not a world *and* the Silence. There is not a relative *and* an Absolute. There is not a "me" and God. There is only one thing. God is all there is.

38. Is the growth of consciousness gradual or sudden?

Actually, growth of consciousness is continuous. You are seeing this from the perspective of the extremely small amount of time since the moment you were born until now. Consciousness exists boundless and complete always and yet awareness of that expands forever. There is a point where identification with the mind as the self is surrendered forever, and this state is traditionally known as Enlightenment. There are periods where seeming "leaps" of consciousness are made, which are sudden, and periods where there is a gradual expansion of awareness, so in another sense, both could be said to be true.

You only get one moment to wake up, and you get it over and over again. There is no point where you have reached some magical destination and are done. Once you have a clear experience of true peace, it is simply a matter of learning to rest there, moment by moment, until the choice is so natural that you just don't leave it.

If you decide that there will be one moment in the future when you can be free, then there is only one chance for you to get it. If you decide to embrace the fact that it always starts now, then you get an infinite number of moments to choose for Truth.

The most incredible thing is that when you clearly begin to discover inner peace, and are willing to rest there, the experience is so fulfilling that the idea of needing to get to some other place is ridiculous. The possibility that there is always more expansion is exciting, yet the experience now is complete in and of itself.

This is a huge step, as it opens the door to grace. The most profound and permanent advancements in consciousness are a result of a movement of grace from within, not because of personal effort. The spiritual path is learning to get out of the way and let the natural return to the Self happen *to* you.

Any efforting and trying on your part keeps the ego in play. With the tiniest amount of effort you are almost home. With no effort at all you are there.

39. Do we have an effect on humanity as we evolve?

Absolutely, the greatest effect. No matter what one's state of consciousness, there is an impact on the rest of creation. Every thought we entertain, every action we take leaves an imprint in consciousness that lasts forever.

As one evolves, that impact increases immensely. Every time one chooses for a higher truth, *that* choice leaves an eternal imprint in consciousness. The choice for higher truth carries a greater weight than the choice for ignorance. Like footprints in the sand, the heavier the walker, the deeper the imprint.

Every person who walks the path of surrender to God leaves a greater knowingness that the path is available for those who follow. It is akin to clearing the brush and thorns away from a walking path, leaving it more visible and easier to navigate for those who come after you.

The further along the path of surrender you walk, the further the path is illuminated, so it is a great service to the awakening of humanity as a whole.

More immediately, every choice you make ripples instantly throughout the universe, because everything is connected in consciousness. The more identified you are with the Absolute, the more impact your choices have. The entire universe responds instantly to praise, gratitude, love, harmony and peace, It literally lights up everything. If someone could just see that, they would never consciously choose for anything else again.

Yes ✔ whole paragraph

More immediately again, most of humanity lives with a whole lot of boundaries, limitations and protective walls around themselves. You are allowed to be happy, but not *too* happy. You can do and be what you want, provided you stay within the confines of what society deems "normal." We live in a mental prison of "what if's," "should's and should not's," and "what would they think's." We don't often praise and encourage those around us, we don't often openly love like there is enough to go around, or meet people without some pre-conceived idea of their value.

As one evolves and lets go of those positions and judgments, automatically we begin to relate to the world around us in a different way. We tend to tell those close to us what they mean to us. We no longer live by a set of imaginary rules and conditions, and the sense that you could do something wrong begins to disappear.

When you meet someone or see a stranger, the previous judgments based on their appearance dissolve, and what is left is the recognition of their innate divinity. Everything is seen as whole and complete, lacking nothing.

Imagine a world where everyone was seen as being worthy of love, needing to change nothing about themselves. Imagine a world where people were held in a space of limitless potential. That would be an amazing world. As you evolve and let go of your own positions and limitations, this is what you begin to bring to *your* world; your family, friends, work colleagues, grocery clerks...everyone.

Whether they notice it consciously or not, whether they react positively or not, just by your presence you have raised the bar, so to speak. You have modeled a way of life dedicated to higher awareness, freedom and love silently and genuinely. This has an enormous impact on everyone. The deepest part of them begins to remember that limitation is *not* natural, even if it appears to be normal. Part of them remembers that they can wake up too.

No matter which way you look at it, waking up is the greatest endeavor. For you, there is an infinite field of love, joy and freedom to experience. As you align more and more completely with that field, you impact everything in creation, backwards and forwards forever by the way, and bring an invitation to freedom to all of those in your immediate sphere of influence. It is the ultimate win/win situation. When one person decides to claim their birthright of eternal peace, everyone benefits.

40. Does enlightenment look a certain way on the outside?

Enlightenment does not necessarily look any particular way on the outside. It is an intensely subjective experience. From that state, the personality will continue in the world as it does. What is constant is that the motive force for continuing to live is Love. The primary desire is to love, rather than to be loved.

A few years ago I was on a teaching tour in Australia. I was in a taxi in Queensland talking with some friends about consciousness when the driver, overhearing the conversation, asked me what I felt was the difference between Elvis and Jesus. It seems like a funny question but it was asked in all sincerity.

Elvis was consumed by the desire to be loved. He wanted to be adored and recognized. His life, although abundant with money, seeming friends, and fame, ultimately was tragic.

Jesus was consumed by the desire to love. Everything he did, he did to serve God, unconditionally, and to have people realize their own freedom. With the love of God as his only point of reference, even in circumstances that would make most people turn away in fright, his life was spectacular.

Love is the motive force of the entire universe; everything is that. Not love as a sensory feeling, but love as an unchangeable state of being. How that looks in its expression is limitless. There are Teachers who are very saintly in their expression, and this is one possibility. There are others who are famously uncompromising in their intolerance of ignorance. Each draws to them those students who need to hear the message in that way.

Two contemporary awakened Teachers of India early in the twentieth century illustrate this. Ramana Maharshi suddenly awakened at an early age. From that one moment on he never left his true nature as consciousness aware. He sat in silence for over twenty years, in bliss.

Seeing his state, many began to come to be with him, simply to sit in his presence. An ashram was built around him, and more and more people came, both Eastern and Western. Everything about him was gentle. Even to look at his picture brings a certain awareness of the sweetest aspects of consciousness. He looks like an angel. When he did speak, his delivery reflected this, and yet he never compromised on the absolute nature of existence.

Another sage was Nisagardatta Maharaj. He was a shopkeeper. He had a Teacher who gave him instruction on Self-realization. He followed it to the letter and became Self-realized. He was implored to teach by those who recognized something of his state. He gave meetings and discourses in a little room above his shop.

He was ruthless in his delivery of truth. To see footage of him even introducing himself to people, it looks as if he will explode at any moment. He constantly drove people to the understanding that nothing of their mind was of any value. Countless people came to see him as they were drawn to the teaching that would serve them at that time.

Both of these sages were awake. Ramana: gentle love. Nisargadatta: ruthless compassion. Yet their inner state was the same.

This is not a way to justify ignorant behavior, but for the student, it is important to know that the mind's idea of how a conscious person would act is never going to be accurate. The mind can know nothing about enlightenment. It is really important to remain aware of the Teaching and how it affects *your* inner experience.

This is also true for those who seem to perfectly embody the mind's idea of enlightenment. Just because somebody wears saffron robes and has a Sanskrit name and is a vegetarian, doesn't mean that they are enlightened. Adolf Hitler was a meditating vegetarian. There are no codes of conduct in consciousness. For the enlightened, there is the direct realization of the Self as the absolute reality of all that is; period.

To find someone who has completely transcended identification with the individual mind is very rare. Even amongst those beings that *do* transcend the mind completely, those who are able to communicate a valid path of return to others are rarer still. For some, waking up was spontaneous and so offering guidance to others can be difficult. For such sages, there is no understanding of how to move beyond the limitations of the mind. For them it just happened.

The truest of teachers are far more concerned with the students experience than their own. The freedom of the student is paramount. You may find that the actions of the teacher serve to show you where you have ideas about what a spiritual life should look like, and let them go.

Removing myself from the world and living in a cave would have been easy for me, even desirable, but my Teacher showed me that this is only half the experience. He showed me how to live 200 percent of life, to bring the presence of God into the world. Had I done it the way my mind wanted to, I would have ended yet another lifetime half-baked, half done. What a waste that would have been.

41. How do your values change as you grow?

At different stages of evolution, different things are important to you. Take, for instance, the need to be right. At a certain level of consciousness, being right, or being *seen* to be right, are very important. As one evolves through cultivating an experience of inner peace, it becomes clear that the need to be right compromises that peace, and so you begin to prioritize peace over right-ness.

This took a long time for me to see. I needed to at least be *seen* to be right to reinforce a pretty shaky sense of self-worth. All of the value that I had was based on the recognition of the outside world. This is a pretty hard way to live, because the outside is constantly changing, and opinions will differ.

As the experience of the silent presence within became clearer, it was obvious that no matter what was occurring outside, I was OK; no matter what was being said, my value was total. There was only love, and that love was dependant on nothing other than my existence. The need to be right became much less appealing than the experience of that presence, and was eventually replaced by it.

As awareness evolves, priorities naturally change. Jealousy and anger are replaced by love and compassion. Sadness and guilt are replaced by presence and forgiveness. As consciousness expands to reveal more of your own innate divinity, the qualities of that experience become prioritized automatically.

We always prioritize things based on our current state of awareness. In the living experience of true freedom, the qualities of love, peace, joy, beauty and truth become fundamental to one's state of being. Service to your fellow man is also a constant priority in an awakened state.

Personal will versus Divine will is another major area where values and priorities change. Once the ego realizes it wants something, whatever that may be, it goes into a frenzy to make it happen. Not just to make it happen, but to make it happen 'my' way.

As one learns to take the awareness inward to Source, there is a great joy in surrendering the outcome to God, surrendering my personal, little, whiny will to a greater will. The desires can be enjoyed, but the attachment to their fulfillment is surrendered. The individual achievement becomes much less fulfilling than surrendering to the perfect unfolding of the universe.

This is not as passive as it sounds. When you are not attached to a particular outcome, there is no sense that you could get it wrong, and so you are much more free to take the steps placed before you to move towards the goal. If the path appears to change course, you are also free just to flow with it.

If you want freedom, peace and joy, those are things that you need to learn to value above all else; discovering those states as a living experience and then prioritizing them over other, less fulfilling states. It really isn't hard. With a little willingness and perseverance, all past habits can be broken, and your life can be lived as it was always intended to be, with a constant awareness of infinite consciousness.

42. Can one fall from this state of awareness or does it remain permanent no matter what?

Oh, it's possible to fall from a high state of consciousness for sure, and it's more common than you would think. Most often it happens as someone moves naturally from a high state to begin to teach others. Teaching is a fairly natural progression, as the experience of consciousness tends to grow rapidly through the willingness to give it away.

The flip side of this is that you can also be presented with the opportunity to claim the state of awareness for the ego. There is the opportunity to take a false sense of personal power. This is the beauty of the path, because there is the continual opportunity to surrender more and more fully to the silent presence within, or not.

The last Maharishi of the Ishaya tradition said very clearly that the choice to surrender everything to divinity becomes more important, not less, as one evolves.

All of the great teachers who came before left a very clear teaching about this. They were all shown the potential personal benefits of claiming power for themselves, even to the point of ruling the world. They also chose to give all glory to God, and in doing so, moved through the final doorways into absolute divinity.

Anywhere you find yourself in a position of helping others discover more of themselves, it carries a huge responsibility. To take personal credit for helping others is, karmically, not a good idea!

Surrender is never difficult, and there comes a point where the experience of the Absolute is so fulfilling that it would seem ludicrous to re-enliven the ego, and yet it is possible.

The formula is always the same; either claim ownership of consciousness for yourself, or surrender everything to God, it's your choice. To unconsciously lead a questing soul away from freedom due to spiritual error is one thing; to *consciously* do this out of some egocentric arrogance is an atrocity.

The good news is that the teacher carries all of the responsibility for the teaching. Any falseness in the teaching through ignorance is not the responsibility of the student. That responsibility lies solely with the teacher.

"Falling from grace," as reclaiming the ego is sometimes called, is not just possible for those who formally teach. At all times in human life there is the possibility of falling asleep, even for a moment. It is as simple as grabbing a thought, or holding a position, without realizing that this is what has happened. When you see it, let it go. None of this is rocket science. Continuing to hold a position is clearly different than surrendering it and returning to peace.

Watch your mind and see where you will reinforce and solidify a position. None of it is present, none of it is freeing, and none of it is even accurate. The longer you hold a position about something or someone, the less validity any of your thoughts around it have, because your mind will change and manipulate your perspectives just to prove the position right.

In order for the experience of the Divine to be permanent, a permanent experience of surrender to that is necessary. The good news is that this path is called "the path of return to freedom," not "the path of never leaving." Whenever you notice that you have grabbed a thought, or have left the experience inner peace, it is simply a matter of letting go and returning to that, without judgment. Approach it all like this and things will be much easier.

Have the humility to ask for help when you need it from those who understand the choice clearly.

Own nothing for yourself and give all glory to God. This is the way. It is an honor and a blessing to be able to choose for your true nature, let alone to be able to share the experience of the divine with others, a humbling privilege. All arrogance is of the ego. In the genuine experience of the silent presence of God, arrogance is not possible actually. Surrender and humility are the very qualities of the Divine.

43. How does one become unconditionally loving?

The way humans normally experience love, or at least our perception of love, is as something to get, something to be acquired. Somewhere along life's winding road, people learn that love is something that you only get when you behave a particular way. We learn not to show the parts of ourselves that we believe to be unworthy and unlovable.

We enter into our relationships on shaky, unspoken contracts where I behave in certain ways to get what I need from you, and you do the same back. This is completely conditional, and I would say is not love at all. It is a fear-based way to get a poor emotional substitute for true love. It is all rooted in taking, rather than giving. There is virtually a 100% focus on what I can get out of the relationship rather than what I can give.

It only happens like this because we have forgotten where love is. We have forgotten that within us is a wellspring of limitless love. When that experience is forgotten, there is no other option than to seek outside of ourselves for love, acceptance and validation.

Beyond a feeling that comes and goes, true love is a constant, unshakeable state of being, *your* being. It is present always. From that experience, I don't love you because you are this way or that way; I just love you because you are. The need for approval dissolves, the need for acceptance dissolves, the desire to have others behave and act in a particular way for us to be happy dissolves.

Even if you *know* intellectually that love can be like that, it doesn't really change anything because it is still a concept. You need to have the *experience*, to discover the source of love for yourself.

Once you begin to see that love is there, within you all the time and not limited in any way, and that nothing about you needs to change to deserve it, then you no longer need anyone else to give it to you. You need do nothing other than let go of the beliefs that tell you that the source of true love exists outside of you, and that you are not quite worthy of it now. As this inner state dawns, you are free for the first time to really love, without conditions.

It becomes automatic to see that there is enough love for everyone, that all people are grounded in the same thing and deserve it equally.

There is only infinite and unconditional love, and the degree to which someone recognizes it or not. So you see that love and compassion are intimately linked, in fact they are the same thing, Love is the essence, compassion is the expression.

44. How can I develop true compassion for myself and others?

Compassion blossoms automatically as consciousness grows. You have always seen the world through your own state of consciousness, through the filters of your own judgments.

If you are fearful or timid, then the world can be a scary place, and the people in it inherently dangerous and threatening. If you are happy and joyful, then the world you live in seems a much more open place, and people too.

As you begin to experience your own perfect divinity, and that you have never done anything wrong, this becomes the platform you see the world from. You will directly see that people are only ignorant of their own divine beauty, which is always there, full and complete. This ignorance is the cause of all suffering.

It becomes obvious that all beings simply desire true happiness, true love, and this motivates all action. Everyone, no matter what his or her race, gender or background, deserves to be free. Everyone deserves to transcend his or her belief in separation from God.

What appears in front of you, in all circumstances, is recognized as Divine. Unconditional love for all of life is the consequence of release of judgment. This is compassion.

As with everything, it has to begin with *you*. The only way to master compassion is to take your awareness inward to its source. Through this inward movement, judgment is surrendered, and separation ends. It is *your own* divinity that you will recognize first.

You are now, and have always been, complete and whole and free. There is only the forgetting or remembering of this. When you see yourself like this, when you see the world like this, miracles are possible. Everyone deserves to be seen like that, to be seen as perfect and whole now. Imagine the power of being seen as needing to fix nothing about yourself to be more acceptable, to be more ready, to be more deserving of love. One glance from a realized being can be enough to dissolve all belief in separation for one who is ready to let go.

45. How can I be free of fear?

All fear, no matter how big or small, is rooted in the belief that you are separate from God. While you live in a separate universe, there is the possibility to the mind that you can be hurt or annihilated, wiped from existence.

This perspective naturally begins to fade with a true spiritual practice. As your experience begins to show clearly that there is nothing outside of you at all, that there is only radiant consciousness, fear dissolves and is replaced by love. More accurately, reality is seen to be as it always was; as love, total and complete. In the experience that there is only God, what or who could fear anything?

Throughout my entire life, from as long ago as I can remember, there was a constant sense of fear. I didn't always *feel* scared, yet the fear was always in play. I was terrified of the dark, of spiders, of sharks, of plane crashes, of people, of endless things. At the root of all of it was a not so subtle fear of death. I was terrified of not existing.

I was always aware of a presence that felt like it was looking over my shoulder, chasing me through life waiting for an opportunity to strike.

After only a short time of meditation, I began to notice places in my life where that fear was no longer in play. It was the biggest shock to me the first time I simply caught a spider and put it outside. The fear began to dissolve quite naturally.

As the experience of the inner silence and peace became constant, the love of that naturally began to replace the fear. Even the presence which I had subtly run from my whole life revealed itself to be nothing other than the presence of God, waiting for me to return home. Now there is the constant and direct experience that existence has no opposite, that I am eternal. It is crystal clear that there is nothing, there is no self outside of the silence.

To be free of fear, to be free of any limitation, it is only necessary to recognize your true nature. It is only necessary to return to union with all that is.

46. How does one live a life of purity when there is so much negativity in the world?

Leave the world's negativity to itself and seek your highest desire. You will discover that, despite the seeming negativity of the world, there is also a world filled with people for whom truth and beauty and divinity are paramount.

Don't let your ego tempt you back into pointing the finger at the world for a reason why you can't do it. "Seek first the Kingdom of Heaven, and all else shall be added unto you." That's what the man said. Make waking up your priority, and you will find yourself in the company of those who want the same thing. You will find techniques and guidance to bring you into the presence of God. Make freedom your first priority, and you may find yourself living in a different kind of world. The actual world doesn't change, but you have only ever seen it through your own mental filters of faulty belief. As those filters change, so the experience of the world changes.

To see the negativity of the world, and be disheartened by it, is actually not a bad first step. Now you have the possibility to make a commitment to yourself to make a difference, but this has to begin and end with you. I will tell you that here and now, your search may very well be over. You are not only hearing about the possibility of freedom; you are being offered a Teaching that will directly bring that to your experience.

What appears to be the world's negativity can, upon examination, be seen to begin and end with your own judgment. You live in a world, the experience of which you are absolutely accountable for. It is not that things can't change, and change for the better, but the heaven or hell you occupy is completely your choice.

By being willing to make that choice and free yourself from self-imposed bondage, you impact the world in ways that are impossible to describe. From that experience of freedom, the things you do to leave the world a better place than you found it have a lasting effect.

Albert Einstein put this simply and beautifully when he said, "No problem has ever been solved from the same level of consciousness that created it."

It is common beginning on a spiritual path to want to leave the world behind. Forever, there have been those that have walked away from the world to be free. Unfortunately, it is really one's own judgments that are being walked away from, and long term this won't work.

"Wherever you go, there you are." No matter how many lifetimes it takes, the desire to be free requires you to transcend judgment, not to run away from it. It is not a difficult thing, when you see that the result of letting your judgments go is eternal peace.

47. What does it mean to be pure?

As with everything on the spiritual path, the mind cannot even begin to comprehend true purity. To the mind it will always be about an outer manifestation. The only way to reach true purity is to rest consciously in the direct experience of your divinity. With all action motivated by that, purity is automatic.

The desire to be pure is a beautiful thing, a worthy thing, and yet the mind's idea of purity often leads to self-violence. Maybe you believe that to be pure you cannot have a coffee in the morning, or that poverty is somehow more pure than living an abundant life. Maybe a fulfilling relationship is something you believe is impure and not in alignment with the will of God. There are a million things that the mind can see as impure, and yet changing the outside is not true purity. Allowing yourself to discover and experience your true self is the only way to become truly pure.

The mind's concepts of purity have also led untold numbers of seekers to align themselves with, and entrust their growth to, teachers who live the ideals of purity to the letter. What is missing, more often than not, is the inner realization of divinity. Without this realization, the value of the guidance for awakening is nil.

All the attributes of consciousness come from experiencing consciousness. The simplest, most direct, and least self-violent way to achieve purity, is to discover your true nature and rest there.

48. What is the difference between pain and suffering?

Most people believe that pain and suffering are the same thing. In another sense however, pain is a sensation and suffering is following the stories associated with it; the anguish and lamentation around why and how the pain occurred. These stories will always be putting the source of the pain outside of you, and this makes you a victim of circumstances. The way out of the suffering, which is actually easy, becomes shrouded and veiled by the mind's self pity.

Pain is an experience that comes and goes, yet funnily enough, so is pleasure. Humanity seeks pleasure to avoid or escape pain. Beyond the feeling of pain and the feeling of pleasure is the reality of Bliss. Pleasure may still come and go, as may pain, and yet the inner state of freedom and bliss is unending. It is not brought about by some outer circumstance, nor is it diminished by it. This experience, letting go of the stories associated with a painful or unpleasant experience, is the end of suffering.

Pain may or may not be an experience in any given moment, but suffering is a story. Telling your self the same story over and over only perpetuates the suffering. Ending suffering is as simple as surrendering the all too familiar stories we hold so dear. When you notice yourself moving into your story, simply let it go. This becomes quicker and quicker with practice and willingness, until you just don't go there any more.

If the idea of suffering still remains in the mind, the mind will be perpetually restless. Once both pain and pleasure are transcended, what remains is bliss, uncaused, and self-perpetuating. It is, in fact, eternal.

49. Why is it so difficult to live in the present moment?

From living our lives identified with thought, the present moment is not something we are really aware of. We are always in another moment, mentally somewhere else in time.

It is only difficult to live in the present moment while we believe the thoughts in our head to be us. In fact, until you have a clear experience of the silent presence of your own consciousness, living in the present is not only difficult, it is impossible.

This is why meditation is so important. It very quickly allows you to see the thoughts as separate from you, and then to discover the witnessing presence, the infinite silent peace of your true nature.

As you become more familiar with that presence, and bathing in it becomes easier, every time you are not experiencing that you have basically grabbed a thought.

"You don't understand, this might happen in the future." Thought. "No, you don't get it, this happened in the past." Thought. "I don't know if I am even experiencing peace; the peace isn't big enough; I don't feel like the peace is me." Thought, thought, thought.

If you really want to live your life in the present, which is a great idea because now is where your life is actually happening, learn to let go of the mind and return to a conscious awareness of the silence beyond it. Practice watching your mind and discovering for yourself the peace of seeing movement as separate from you. As you watch, effortlessly and innocently, the presence becomes increasingly apparent, and appealing. Allow it to open to you, allow it to come to you.

You will see for yourself that all of the problems you have exist solely in your mind, and that they take you away from the experience of now. It's not that challenges go away, but problems always exist in your head. In this moment you don't have a problem. In this moment there is peace. In this moment you are free.

50. I heard a teacher recently talk of levels of enlightenment and referred to the enlightenment of the body. What is that?

The body will respond to an increase in consciousness, and yet in and of itself, it cannot become enlightened. You may notice stronger feelings of joy or bliss, and stronger levels of energy. Sometimes this can be almost painful as the body takes on a greater level of spiritual "current" than it has held before, but these are simply experiences along the way. They are not even common to all, are not necessary and are certainly not enlightenment of the body.

Almost all the spiritual seekers of the world are chasing these kinds of experiences. Without the guidance of those who have realized their true nature as pure consciousness, the mind will go on chasing sensory experiences and feelings for a sign of progress, and yet it is all a distraction. It can be a way for the mind to maintain control of your path.

Enlightenment is only of the consciousness. It is the recognition and direct experience that the Self is beyond the mind, beyond the body, beyond anything that can be experienced with the senses. To talk of the body as enlightened is like talking about how much your car enjoyed the drive over here. It is simply a vehicle to get you around.

Yes, it's great to have a nice one, or to look after it, but in and of its self it is not conscious. It *responds* to consciousness.

Your experience of the world will change as you grow, but this is not the body becoming enlightened. Even if you wake up one day and a life long condition has healed, or your eyesight improves, all of which have happened to people as they become more conscious, this is simply the body's response to consciousness.

The flip side of this is that even if your body doesn't heal, or your eyesight gets worse, this is not necessarily a sign that you are not conscious. As has already been stated, enlightenment is completely subjective. It is a reality that cannot adequately be described, nor displayed, and yet everything that occurs from that realization occurs spontaneously. All investment in outcome is surrendered and everything is experienced as a direct consequence of the presence of God.

51. How is it possible to experience inner peace in the midst of so much outer turmoil and chaos?

It is possible when you discover how easy it is to experience true peace. Just the recognition of the presence of peace is enough. You can directly experience that right now, you can be still, and there is peace.

The mind may say, "Yes I can rest in the experience of peace now, but when I get home it is going to be so much harder."

"Yes, I can do it now, but what about when you look on television and see what the real world is like?"

All of these are arguments against the absolute reality that in every moment peace exists. I have never met anyone who had a good argument against the Absolute reality. Once you see these excuses, and your belief in them, you have identified false idols, the things you make more real than the presence of God.

The degree to which you can see this and surrender the excuses, is the degree to which you actually want what you say you do, and consequently, is also the degree to which you will experience peace. This is "walk your talk" time.

Things that seem to disturb you only have the power you give to them. Initially, forget about making the experience of true peace permanent; simply rest there when you remember. You only have one moment to choose, and that moment is now. This is why innocence is so important.

Innocently coming back to the presence of peace now, whenever you notice you have left it, opens you to being filled up, rather than trying to cram it into your day on your agenda. True peace is completely beyond space and time. Trying to fill up a mind-created twenty four hours with peace is arrogant, actually. The divine presence exists in eternity; the minutes of your day exist only in your mind. The two are mutually exclusive.

As you innocently give yourself to the present moment, what that moment really is begins to expand and stretch. If you let it, it will devour the mind's ideas of time and space and reveal itself to you as it truly is: timeless and omnipresent; one unmoving, eternal moment.

CHAPTER 5

Spiritual Practice – Walking the Talk

For most people in the world today, the ideas of spiritual growth, expansion of consciousness or enlightenment are completely foreign. There is no context within which to experience such things, so going through life trying to get whatever joy is possible before death is most people's concept of the natural state.

Once one realizes that there is potentially a much bigger purpose to life, the search begins for ways to discover this, and experience the True Nature of the Self.

As we begin to search we are bombarded with a multitude of different religions, paths, beliefs and tools, all of which claim to bring one to the goal of human life. Interestingly, what that goal is can be radically different depending on which path or teaching you listen to.

All of these things have their own value. Each of them can, and does, bring a particular level of fulfillment to those that are drawn to them, and yet for the one who knows that the purpose of life is to awaken from the dream completely, the choice of which path to walk or which tool to use, becomes narrower and narrower. The promises of healing power, the singing of devotional songs or achieving rigorous physical postures, no longer have the same fulfillment, simply because, as beautiful as they may be in their own right, they will always fall short of the goal. It is so easy to become enamored with the path, and to feel proud of the things we do to move closer to our hearts desire.

The practice itself, whatever it may be, is *not* the goal.

The goal of awakening to the presence of God is ultimately simple and direct. Therefore, any tool that could be of value must also be simple and direct.

As one evolves, spiritual practice must also necessarily evolve. All spiritual practice has benefits; all spiritual practice meets the need of a particular level of spiritual awareness. Very few spiritual practices meet the need of the smallest number of aspirants; those who seek freedom from the limited mind, and union with God, above all else.

52. I am a beginner at all of this and have no idea where to start. What advice can you offer?

Know what it is that you want. When you know that, everything else gets supremely simple. You know you want to wake up because you are here. You know that what keeps you from freedom is your identification with your mind. Knowing that, find something that will help you change your relationship with your mind.

If what you have seen and heard here resonates with your desire to be free, then try this practice and see if it brings you what you desire. If this does not resonate with your desire to be free, then find something that does.

Either way, there is nothing specific that you need to understand to experience your heart's greatest desire. There is no knowledge that is required. For you, the path is remembering how to let go.

As far as feeling like a beginner, remain like that. I don't mean to remain feeling like you need to do more or figure something out to be free, but remain in the innocence of simply exploring what you already have. Do not allow yourself to get to a place where you feel like you have obtained something special, something you did not have before, or something that others don't have.

When you simply allow yourself to be here, completely in this moment without any regret for the past or fear for the future, you will experience the presence and the peace you have thirsted for your entire life. Discover that as a living experience, and dedicate your life to exploring and surrendering more of yourself to it.

You are not a beginner because you are already free, you just forgot for a little while. The good news is the remembering has already begun.

53. I am interested in spirituality, but what if my friends and family think I am weird?

There are a couple of things about that. I don't know your friends and family, but it is always wise to be discerning about what you tell people. It's not that you have this big secret or anything like that, but people are only willing and able to hear so much.

Even though for you, your practice may be about discovering your true nature and developing an awareness of infinite silence, it may be that what you share with those close to you is that you are learning meditation so that you can find more peace. This is still true, but it is just a little easier to understand for those who know nothing about the path.

One thing is for sure, if you are sharing anything but your *experience* of your path, then you can get into conflict with others, because it will be belief systems competing for dominance. If you are just sharing your heart, your joy then even if it is not completely understood by the others, there is usually not much room for conflict.

Another angle on this is that you have lived your entire life basing, at least to some degree, your sense of self-worth on what other people think. This leads to a less than satisfactory life. How long you want to live like that is up to you. You don't need to alienate yourself from the people in your life that you love and care for, but if there is something that is important to you, why would you deny it just because someone else thinks it's weird? You will end up not living your life's purpose, and resenting your loved ones all at the same time.

Ultimately, you are embarking on a path of increasing joy, peace and love. The patterns in your mind that have made your relationships less than enjoyable are going to dissolve. If you discover your true nature, you will become a better partner, parent and friend. You are going to discover the wellspring of true love that exists within you. Who wouldn't want that for you?

As you move into an awareness of peace and let go of limiting judgments, people notice it, and more often than not, are attracted to the state of freedom you are developing. Many times it is those close to us who notice the positive changes before we do.

I was talking to a guy in Dublin, Ireland a few years ago. He had been meditating for a while, and was saying to me he was thinking of giving it up. Out of the kitchen his wife's voice came booming, "Michael, if you stop meditating I'm divorcing you!"

She saw the beneficial changes in him, even though *he* didn't in that moment.

There is nothing negative about Self-discovery. You are leaving behind the false to discover the real. There are those who would prefer you to remain small and limited, because then they are not challenged to change themselves, but really, who wins then?

A great teacher once said, "Life is meant to be lived in eternal joy, Infinite freedom, Unconditional love and unbounded awareness. Any other life is utterly missing the point of being born as a human."

At the end of the day, what you make of your life is your choice. When this life ends, you will only be accountable to yourself. How much you lived your dreams, or how much you compromised on them will be the only thing that matters.

54. How does one witness the mind?

Simply begin it. You only know you think because part of you is aware of the fact, so observation is, to some degree, already happening. The thing that stops it being a clear experience is that a thought flows through the mind and you believe that you are actually thinking it. What is even worse than that, the content of the thought seems personal and so you believe that the thought determines who you are.

By simply being willing to rest and allow thought to move, part of you recognizes that you and the thoughts are separate. This can be a daunting thing initially, but with clear guidance from someone who knows, it becomes easy very quickly to distinguish between you as the *witness* of the thoughts and the thoughts themselves. Then your attention can gently, and easily be brought into awareness of what it is that is observing.

It is one thing to know that you observe. It is another thing altogether to consciously experience the quality that is called awareness. This takes you to a level where the presence or absence of thought is irrelevant to your state of being. Witnessing the mind is only the first step.

teaching meditation

You can begin by simply taking some time each day to close your eyes, and simply be aware of the thoughts as they flow through the mind. It can be easier in the beginning to actually count the thoughts, to give everything that moves in your awareness a number, although ultimately this is unnecessary. Simply relax, and watch. It doesn't matter if you get caught on a thought here and there. When you notice that you are thinking, simply rest back, let your attention be wide and watch again. After only a few moments you will begin to notice a peace within, a quality of stillness.

As simple as witnessing sounds, and it is simple, guidance is key. A technique that will allow you to become increasingly aware of the inner presence is also a blessing. Years ago, I was reading an excerpt from a book about quantum physics. As I was reading, something leapt off the page at me. It said something along the lines that it had been proven that the observer creates the observed. This awed me because what that meant was that if all I knew about meditation was to observe the mind, then I could create a mind forever to observe! It was a self-fulfilling thing, and it was a trap.

I have met people who have meditated like this for years, simply watching. They are veritable mind watching masters and yet for most of them, there is not a solid recognition of their true nature, and certainly not an on-going one.

It is in the observing of movement that the identification with movement is surrendered. From there, it is possible to shift *all* attention into the field of awareness itself. Identification with that field of consciousness alone is freedom.

55. How does one go about stilling the mind?

Have you ever tried to still the mind? For most people I have ever spoken with, this is the reason they shy away from spiritual practice. There is a core belief that, in order to experience divine peace, the mind must be permanently stilled. This is putting the cart before the horse.

The greatest of sages have known forever that it is not necessary to still the mind to discover peace. They have always said, "Discover peace first, and the mind naturally stills."

Peace is constant, stillness is constant, and God is constant. These things have no opposite. It is simply the belief that we need to do something more to discover peace that keeps us from the experience now...and now is the only time you will ever be able to experience it, ever.

Simply by resting, and allowing yourself to be aware without effort, you will begin to discover the silence within.

Instead of trying to stop thoughts, or force a gap so you can find the space between them, simply relax and discover the space within which the thoughts arise. Like the words on a page, if you want to discover the white of the page, you can try to focus very hard on the space between the letters, and probably go cross eyed, or you can simply rest a little, and allow yourself to discover the space, the page, upon which the words appear. This is only an analogy, and a beginning.

Your relationship to the mind can be approached in this way too. Many practices teach that one should try to find the gap between two thoughts. This can be done, but there is an easier way. By allowing the thoughts to be there without investment, you can begin to discover the space, the field of awareness, within which the thoughts appear. It is not necessary to put great effort into stilling the movements of the mind.

It is funny actually to talk of stilling the mind, when the part that appears to move is so tiny. You can experience this easily: that the majority of the mind is already still. The mind, true mind, is literally infinite, and only the tiniest, tiniest part appears to move at all. No matter how much thought and movement there appears to be, put your attention on the part of the mind that is already still. You may just discover that nothing was ever really moving in the first place.

It is simply a shift of attention from content to context. For you to be aware of any object, there must be space for it to exist in. For you to be aware of any sound, there must be silence for it to exist in. For you to be aware of any form, there must be formlessness for it to appear in. Somehow, we have learned to focus only on the *content*, only on the movement, only on the changing, only on the form. Here, we are learning to discover the unmoving, unchanging *context* of all experience.

Ultimately, you can discover awareness *prior* to the arising of thought, and in that there is no movement, ever.

56. How do I live permanently in the present moment and not the past or future?

The short answer is don't follow a thought! Every thought has one common element...time. Every thought is either about the past or the future, even the ones that appear to be present.

Even in meditation, there are thoughts that are continually commenting on your experience. "Wow it's really still in here," "This stillness is amazing," or, "This is really boring, I can't sit here for one more minute." These commentating voices seem to be giving you valid information on your experience in the present moment, but in fact, the experience they are telling you about is already gone. They are commentating on how it was just an instant before. Your awareness has already left the present moment and is peeking back at how it was, and talking about it. Not only that, but when the voice in your head talks to you about your experience, you talk back.

The voice says, "This is really boring." And then you say, "Yes it is, shall we go and watch TV for a while?"

It is such a fascinating thing, and simply by being willing not to engage the commentator in your head, you will discover for yourself that it has no valid information about the present moment at all.

Every time you actively engage in thinking, you leave the awake reality of now, and fall asleep into dreams and fantasies of the past and the future.

Make a game of it. All day today you can think about the future, but do not consciously think about the past. The thoughts of the past may arise, or you may unconsciously go there, but when you notice you are doing it, stop.

Then, tomorrow, do the same thing with the future. All day tomorrow you can think about the past, but do not consciously think about the future. Don't get frustrated, just play.

It is fascinating to see how much of the day we dwell on one or the other. Some people are habitually past thinkers, some people are habitually future thinkers. Some people just spend the day flitting between one and the other. Becoming aware of the way your mind has conditioned itself to operate gives you everything you need to see it for what it is, and let go of your attachment to it.

If you really want to experience and live from the present moment, the only way is to investigate and change your relationship with your mind, because it is identification with the movements in the mind that pulls you out of your glory.

The present moment is always rich and full. There is always an innocent wonder and awe at the unfolding perfection of now. Any other experience is born simply of identification with thought. As thought is never present, it is automatically dead. If you want to live your birthright of eternal peace and wonder, if you want your life to be continually rich and alive, transcending the mind is the key.

57. What practical changes can be made to effectively serve growth?

The first and most important thing is to cultivate a daily spiritual practice, and specifically a practice of meditation. I can't emphasize enough how important that is. It is important because, not only will it reveal to you the nature of your mind, and give you the opportunity to transcend it, but it also gives you a consistency of focus.

If you want to wake up, it is not enough to be focused once in a while. This is the equivalent of going to church on Sunday and forgetting about God for the rest of the week. With a daily practice of an effective meditation, transcending the habits of negativity and separation can be swift.

There is no other change you could make that will serve your growth more than this. Changing your diet, your exercise regime, your circle of friends all can, and do, have an effect on your focus and growth, but it is minimal compared to developing a regular meditation practice.

With the deep rest that meditation provides, the body can release the stress that has accumulated over your lifetime. This healing allows the nervous system to return to its intended way of functioning; as a vehicle for divinity to express itself. The release of physical and emotional stress is just the beginning.

The experience that you are separate from God is a belief. All inner turmoil and pain is there because of identification with a thought. To know that, or believe that, doesn't help anything. To be free you need to *experience* it, and change your relationship to your mind. The most effective way to discover the nature of reality is to meditate. It allows you to create distance from the movements of the mind, and through that distance, to discover the perfect clarity and silence of your own consciousness.

Many people go about their spiritual growth backwards, putting the cart before the horse, so to speak. They will become vegetarian, take up yoga, start reading spiritual material or put a statue of a saint in the hallway before even considering taking up meditation. It all makes them feel better, and of course provides an environment where they are remembering something greater is possible, but none of it will wake someone up from their dream of a separate existence.

You can do all those things, but separation is experienced simply because you grabbed a thought, and in doing so created the illusion of a limited, individual "me." The only way to right the balance between you and a thought is to see the mind for what it is, and discover that the content of thought is *not* you. The fastest way to discover this is through an effective meditation, and the guidance of those who have discovered this too.

58. What is meant by, "All problems begin and end with me?"

It sounds very mystical doesn't it? All your problems, and in fact all the worlds' problems, have one common factor...you. Not the *real* you, but the little you that is in judgment, and through that judgment creates the illusion of a problem.

The mind is very good at telling the Absolute where it could have done better. It is like the ego believing there is some kind of cosmic suggestion box for God where we can leave our feedback on how she could do better. "I know Lord that you are the omnipotent Creator of all that is, but I think you really messed up here."

It is our own petty judgments that perpetuate separation and cause us pain. Once you learn to let these judgments go, to see them for what they are, automatically separation dissolves.

For me, my judgments of the world were intense. I didn't know how to go on living in the world with all of those problems. It all seemed too hard. The simple fact was that it wasn't the world I was sick of living with, it was me, the small me. My mind was a constant tirade of thoughts, and many of them were about how messed up everything on this planet was. Because I believed I created the thoughts, I also believed that their content, what they were telling me, was true.

As soon as I made the choice that I wanted to be free of my own belief in separation, to wake up from my own crazy dream, the universe moved with amazing speed to bring that to me. Everything just lined up. Actually it became apparent that it was already all lined up, I was just so busy staring down the length of my pointer finger at the world that I couldn't see it.

All I had to do was shift my attention. It took a little remembering, but I had the support, you see? I had the support because I was willing to just go for it and see what happened. That is my recommendation to you...don't take it on board as a conceptual truth, think about it, believe it, or anything like that. Simply begin to apply it to your own experience and see what happens...it's worth it, it's worth everything.

59. What is the value of traditional prayer?

Praying has a huge value. There have been many scientific studies done that show prayer has an effect on the well being of the one being prayed for. There are also uncountable anecdotal accounts of the impact, large and small, of prayer. The results are not affected by which particular faith or tradition the person praying belongs to either. Prayer is a great service if it is directed towards improving or serving one's fellow man.

The impact of prayer, however, is diminished in direct proportion to the personal investment in the outcome of the one praying. The most powerful form of traditional prayer leaves the outcome to God, as you perceive God to be.

There are other ways that the impact of prayer is diminished. Did you ever pray like this? "Lord, get me through this hangover and I swear, I will never drink again!" Or, "Lord, just let me win the lottery, and I promise I will do something really good for humanity." These aren't necessarily the highest forms of intent, and are rarely without personal investment in the outcome.

Another thing with prayer is the amount of time during the day one can spend praying. If prayer is an action that you do, most of the day will necessarily be taken up doing other things.

It is possible, however, for your whole life to *become* a prayer, to live your life in a constant state of surrender to divine will. As you discover the silent presence within, every moment aware of that presence is lived in a state of praise, gratitude and love, and all outcomes are surrendered to God. It does not have to take a long time for that silent, divine presence to become a virtually seamless experience.

This is what is meant by, "praying without ceasing." It is not a constant state of inner chatter where you are the intermediary between the rest of mankind and the infinite; it is a state of silent awareness where everything that enters that field is surrendered back to the will of the Divine.

For most people who are actively involved in prayer, when someone they know or love comes into their awareness, they will verbalize some kind of prayer for that person. It is not just limited to someone they know or love, but it may be a place on Earth that has experienced a tragedy, or any number of other worthy causes.

While these prayers have an effect and really do help, the best thing you can do is surrender your individual awareness of the "problem" to God. If you have an experience of the silence within, surrendering everything that comes into your awareness to that is the highest and most effective form of prayer.

This state also amplifies the effect of traditional prayer. The more immersed in inner presence you become, the greater the impact of your attention. The more free of identification with the mind you are, the greater the impact of your prayer.

None of this is saying that prayer is wrong; it is amazing and powerful. If you really want to have the greatest impact from prayer, surrender everything to God. Do you think God has missed something? Do you think that God has lost control in some way? Do you think God needs reminding of exactly what is happening for anyone anywhere? You cannot determine the will of God, or how to surrender to it from the mind. You have to cultivate an *experience* of that presence so that you have something to surrender to.

Ultimately, the only personal desire left in that state is a wordless expression, "How can I be of service?" and that is the greatest of prayers.

60. How is "one-pointed-ness of mind" attained?

To cultivate one-pointed-ness of mind is the purpose of meditation. Through the constant identification with the mind's endless thought streams, we have become anything but one pointed. In fact, our minds are scattered. The average person's experience is a constant movement of identifying with random thought streams, all of which they believe are created by them. The mind is often likened to a monkey moving from branch to branch in a ceaseless, restless movement. Most people spend their days in a constant dialogue with a myriad of different voices in their head.

With attentiveness and practice, the mind can return to its natural state of one–pointed attention on the presence of God. It doesn't have to take a long time and the more innocent you can be, the faster it is done.

The identification with the surface movement of the mind takes so much energy to maintain. It has been said that the average person thinks somewhere between 90,000 and 100,000 thoughts every day. The number is not important, but this barrage of movement is a direct reflection of the energy needed to maintain separation from the infinite silence that exists just beyond the mind.

Through a valid practice of meditation, the awareness is brought mechanically into contact with this silent presence. As the frenetic energy of separation is let go of, awareness gently rests more fully in that silence. It is actually the natural state of the mind to be still, and so with not much effort at all, stillness becomes recognized as the desired state until it is the only state consciously chosen for. This is one-pointedness. It is not a forceful or effortful thing; it is simply the conscious attention falling in love with its own source.

The interesting thing is that, as this one-pointedness of attention develops inwardly, it is automatically reflected outwardly. This means that it is possible, and in fact easy, to have an ongoing experience of silence with the eyes open. Through this, the experiences and challenges of life are met with more focus, clarity and energy. Every area of life becomes more effective as one releases judgment and the addiction to scattered thought.

The very idea of one-pointedness sounds effortful. It actually requires you to become effort*less*. We have become conditioned to live our lives with 100 percent effort and zero attention. One-pointedness is correcting this imbalance to live life with 100 percent attention and zero effort. This is the natural state; this is the key to permanent peace.

61. What is the difference between worship and meditation?

That depends on *how* you worship, or *how* you meditate. There need not be a difference. Worship, in terms of devotion and surrender to God, is not different from meditation. Meditation, in terms of devotion and surrender to God, is worship.

To truly worship God, rituals and external trappings are not required. The highest form of praise is imitation. The highest form of worship is to unite with the direction of the worship itself.

The purpose of meditation as I am speaking about it here, is to unite with the true beloved, to unite with God. The separate individual you was never real. The purpose of your life is to discover this as your own experience. This is the ultimate value of meditation, and this is also the highest form of worship.

In the beginning for people, whether it is through meditation or worship, the goal is seen as outside of them. It is an object. To worship or be devoted to something outside of you perpetuates separation and the possibility of pain and suffering. Through practice and surrender, the goal becomes discovered as the *subject*, or in other words, "You *are* that which you seek."

So, meditate and discover the presence of perfect silence within you. Recognize and be devoted to the divine perfection all around you, and surrender all experience to that. The discovery of divine glory emerges swiftly when all aspects of life are devoted to God as a living experience, within and without.

62. What are the best qualities a spiritual aspirant should have?

Believe it or not, the willingness to take nothing seriously is paramount. Not many paths teach this, but it is absolutely necessary. You can only take seriously that which you take personally. If nothing is taken personally then it is the smallest step to the experience of the limitless, impersonal Self.

As humans, we tend to take everything so seriously, and this is actually counter-productive to growth of consciousness. The most important thing you can do is to commit to your freedom, but it is not serious.

Jesus said it perfectly, "Unless you are as little children you will not see the Kingdom of Heaven." Be innocent, be gentle with yourself, and take nothing seriously. This is good advice. In fact, as you begin the inner journey you are going to see the foundation of your ego, all the things you believed to be true which are actually not, and that can be embarrassing if you don't have a sense of humor about it!

Beyond that, a little tenacity is not a bad thing either. Remaining committed, no matter what, to realizing the goal of human life. Never give up. The mind will say, "You're not getting anywhere with this. You'll never make it," but these are just the voices of past habit. You just keep going, you just keep moving.

Once you have even entertained the possibility of enlightenment, there is no other outcome possible. It is absolutely certain, and so you just keep going. You immerse yourself in this moment completely. You rest in the silent presence of this moment and it will fill up your consciousness until it lasts forever. It is never somewhere else, simply here now. Stay open and alert.

The last Maharishi of the Ishaya tradition, Sadashiva, wrote, "Whatever it takes, this is the only attitude that will work." Once you know this is what you want, find those who have walked the path before you and go for it with your heart, mind, body and soul.

63. What is the value of guidance?

It could be said that guidance is everything. The form that guidance takes may vary from moment to moment, but it is everything. You may find this very difficult to believe, but it is not possible for the mind to guide you to the Absolute, simply because it needs your attention elsewhere. Everything about the mind is past and future. Everything about the Absolute is here and now. The mind cannot guide you to it because it can never, ever experience it.

Once you have guidance from those who have walked the path before you, it is more valuable than gold. It is everything. That guidance will change your experience forever. On the path to recognizing your true divinity, the experience of the mind can become increasingly subtle, and so those who know this can help you to transcend all of it.

Guidance changes as you grow. At first, you may read a book and get inspired to walk the path to awakening. Later, you may get to be in the presence of teachers who inspire you, offering you tools and guidance that will help you transcend the mind and fan the flame in your heart that longs to be free. Then, at some point you may be in the presence of someone who will do whatever it takes to have you realize your true nature, someone who can walk you through the last of your separation. The point is to continually be open to more and more as you grow.

Your universe will always mirror your commitment, and you will always be asked to accept the invitation for more. The Presence of God is autonomous in that it has no opposite and no argument against it holds any water, yet it is infinitely patient and allows you to take your own way. The outcome is the same; the journey is up to you.

It is not possible for the mind to think its way out of hell, because it is by the mind alone that you entered. You can find the limit of the mind and then surrender that to its source, and the easiest way to do that is with some kind of external guidance. In fact, I would say that it is the only way.

As one begins to move beyond identification with the mind, experiences come to awareness that can be both exciting and unnerving. Having the guidance of one who knows these from their own experience dispels doubt and keeps one on the straight and narrow path. It is easy to be distracted by experiences that are not the goal. Without guidance from someone who has reached the Absolute, these experiences can delay realization for years, even lifetimes.

To find yourself in the presence of one who has awakened is rare. It requires commitment on your part to actually want what you say you want. It is one thing to say, "I want to know myself fully." It is another thing entirely to make that your number one priority. Rarer still is the student who finds themselves in the presence of a Teacher, and is then willing to apply the teaching and surrender fully to the guidance on offer.

It requires nothing more from you than the willingness to continue. As your experience grows and your desire grows, so you will attract to you the guidance necessary to move deeper and deeper into the heart of God. Simply stay open.

64.
I can be aware of stillness and peace quite a lot during my days, but there are certain times where I always lose it. How can I maintain it even in those circumstances?

The easiest way is to practice being aware of presence when there are no challenges directly in front of you. I know you already do that to some degree, but being even more attentive when you can is a key thing. If you can consciously recognize the ease and fulfillment in resting in silence when you are able, it becomes easier and easier to remember in more challenging times.

While it sounds simple, it is actually a radically different approach. In the question you asked there is more of a focus on what you are *not* able to do rather than what you *are* able to do. Give yourself credit for the progress you have made. This allows the experience to fill up more of your days automatically, instead of you feeling like you need to cram the stillness in!

If there are circumstances where you know you habitually react and lose yourself, then these can become a conscious place of practice. If it is always when your mother in law visits then you know, next time she is pulling into your driveway, that you need to be actively alert. If it is always when somebody cuts you off in traffic, then you know when you get into your car, this is a time when you can be actively more alert.

In the alertness, you will notice the habitual energy of reacting beginning to arise, and you can let it go. You will more readily see the thoughts around the person or circumstance that make you react, and you will be able to let them go.

Even if you begin to react, if your ego begins to flare up, you will be more able to watch this happen, and in doing so, will not be so easily swept up in the tide of unconsciousness.

It sounds like you are very aware of certain places where you become unconscious, and most people are really. Rather than seeing these as places where you are "not getting it," make them a major part of your spiritual practice. Prepare yourself to be resting more fully in stillness, to be more aware of your inner presence at those times.

The worst thing you can do is judge yourself for becoming unconscious. You don't do it on purpose, and so it is not your fault. Have you ever been reading a book late at night, and then suddenly awakened in the small hours of the morning with the light still on and the book lying open on your chest?

It is not much different than that. One moment you are aware and alert, and the next, through no fault of your own, you are asleep. As much as possible, don't judge yourself for something you, so far, have no control over. See it as an opportunity when the circumstance presents itself, and growth of awareness will be swift.

65. Is it really as easy as "just being present?"

It depends on what you want. Most of us live our lives with our attention on nothing more than things. Outwardly, our world is all things; possessions, relationships, careers and so on. Unfortunately, this is true inwardly also. Thoughts and feelings take up our whole attention. Being present, for most of us, even if the possibility enters into our awareness, is simply a mental recognition. One recognized snippet of forever is the closest the mind can come to being present.

The mind recognizes only the passage of time, and moments are isolated droplets of this. It is impossible for the waking state mind to be in the eternal Now, simply because everything it experiences is, at best, an instant old.

This is actually not being present at all. To be present one must go beyond the mind. To discover the space that all things come from, all things exist in, and to which all things return is to begin to discover what it truly means to "just be." Just beyond the chatter and movement of the mind, there is a silent field of awareness within which all things appear. From there, it is not far to experience that you and the field are one and the same thing, and that the moment itself is eternal.

The idea the mind has of the present moment is always limited. It seems so incredibly fleeting. The truth is, it is the *things* that are fleeting; your life and everything in it. The moment is actually forever, not fleeting at all, not even moving. What is the quality of awareness? What is it that is aware? What are you? Find out...this is the purpose of your life.

It is a popular thing in spiritual circles to talk about the present moment and "just being." While the essence is correct, it can also be a trap. It is possible to "just be" stuck in any limitation. It is possible to "just be" in the thought that "I am God," which is to "just be" mentally enlightened. This falls indescribably short of the direct experience of selfless All-ness.

You *are* the moment; your awareness is eternal. You are the unborn, undying, fathomless, silent witness of eternity. Discover this and you will find freedom. Discover this as a direct experience and you have lived your life's purpose.

66. Are there any special diets, postures or breathing techniques required to wake up?

No. All these things may help in terms of focus and motivation, but what you seek you already are. Nothing needs to be added to or changed about you in order to "get it." In fact, what is required is only to remove the idea that you are a separate entity. To take away the idea that, because your body is sick or your hair is blue or you watch television, that you are somehow further away from God than anyone else. Or to remove the idea that because you *don't* watch television or eat meat or have sex that you are somehow closer to God than anyone else. It is necessary to let go of all ideas. There is a seduction of the spiritual path known as the spiritual ego, and it is possible for you to fall in love with it.

The ego loves to measure and compare. You can measure how you are doing with thoughts like, "I'm almost there now." "I'm closer to it than I was yesterday, I'm much further along than Bob, but Mary is more enlightened than me." All of it is an attractive denial of the present. The mind is so filled with things that have nothing whatsoever to do with now. All that is required is to give up any other moment than now, simply give it up.

There is also the belief that all you have to do is simply "be." It is possible to just "be" completely caught in the same boundaries that you were yesterday or the day before. To simply be aware of your self is only the first step. The next is to be aware of "who" it is that is aware, and ultimately "what."

All of life is divine and the realization is always subjective. Hold no positions, this is the best advice I was ever given by my Teacher. It hit me in the face like a brick, and yet it was the doorway to the experience I had thirsted for my entire life. This is not an excuse for ignorant behavior, simply an acknowledgement that it is consciousness alone that is the source and goal of life.

So many people I know are more concerned with getting their body in the right position, or shopping at the right book store, or going to the most popular teacher, that they lose track of what they were looking for in the first place.

There was a great teacher in India named Nisargadatta Maharaj, who devoted his life to sharing his experience with all who came. He smoked 80 cigarettes a day as he was teaching. He continually said to people, "The body still has some habits, but listen to the teaching." And the teaching was absolutely pure. This is not to say start smoking, or eating meat, but simply to say that your freedom does not wait for anything, except your willingness to accept it.

If you currently smoke or eat meat, you are no further behind any other human being in your search for true happiness and peace. Beyond all the boundaries of the mind lies a field of infinite potential, and you are that. Embrace it now and live in limitless bliss. Deny it now and delay it for another moment in the future, the choice is yours.

67. What if I don't have the time to meditate or practice spirituality?

You have time to be aware. You can actually make time to meditate if you choose to. It is simply a matter of closing your eyes for a few minutes a couple of times a day, but our days are so filled with stuff that we usually don't make it a priority. In fact, most people don't even want to see if it could become a priority. There are some excellent techniques that make meditation easy and enjoyable, and they can also be used with the eyes open as you go about your day. They will fit with any schedule. The belief that you don't have time is a belief merely, but at the very least, you do have time to practice awareness.

Your life can be your spiritual practice. In fact, it has always been like that, you just haven't seen it that way. In any moment you can be aware of yourself, and rest into the experience of your own presence, innocently and gently aware of the fact that right now...you are. This is the only thing you can ever truly know, the fact that right now in this moment, you exist. Recognizing that, and opening to it you can discover inner peace.

When you notice that you have drifted away, you simply come back again, staying open, like air. With alertness, you will see what it is that you will leave the experience of peace for. You will see that to leave peace is actually a conscious choice. Once you see it, you can begin to choose differently, until a new habit is formed. Stress is the habit of a lifetime, but with only a little willingness it can be undone.

Even though it is the most simple of things, it is so easy to make it conceptual. Without a tool and guidance, the whole journey can become a subtle loop in the mind. Even as you have realizations, these can become no different to other thoughts. Meditation is invaluable. Guidance is invaluable. There are practices of meditation that will fit with every schedule. If you are serious about waking up, about discovering the limitless potential that lies within you, then find one. To say you want the goal and yet proclaim you have no time is an excuse.

68. How do I turn my attention inward?

The concept of inward and outward focus can be misleading. It is more a matter of resting. Simply relaxing back into yourself as though you are resting into a warm bath. For just a moment, let your mind do whatever it wants, and allow yourself to be aware of your own presence as you rest. This is really turning your attention inward. This is opening to the presence of God.

You can say it is inward because usually we have all our attention on what appears to be outside of us, on constant movement and chatter. By simply allowing it to be as it is, without your involvement, automatically you can begin to become aware of your inner experience. With alertness, innocence and practice you will begin to see more and more subtle levels of what is actually outside of you. It will begin to include thoughts and feelings too, and the presence of your true Self consequently becomes clearer.

Meditation is perfect for this. Its purpose is to surrender the movement to the experience of stillness now. With a valid practice of meditation, all boundaries, all positions, all separation can be surrendered and transcended.

69. What does it mean to surrender to the will of God?

In order to know what it means to surrender to the will of God, one must first have a subjective experience of the presence of God, consciously. In the initial stages, this is not the case. If one is trying to learn to surrender to the will of God, then it will only be a mind-projected version of God that we will surrender to. This ultimately means that you will be surrendering to your mind, and this has never gotten anyone very far.

What needs to happen is to learn to observe the movements of the mind. Once you begin to see thought as separate from you, you are automatically no longer claiming ownership of it. This is surrender to God. No longer claiming for yourself that which emanates spontaneously from the infinite field of pure consciousness

It all boils down to a case of mistaken identity. The vast majority of humanity believes that it is the content of the mind, the thoughts and the feelings. When you believe that you are the creator and author of the thoughts and feelings, surrender is impossible. You will proudly claim that which you judge to be good, and out of guilt and shame hide that which you judge to be bad. Neither brings freedom, both are the cause of bondage and separation.

On honest investigation however, it can be clearly experienced that the *real* you is simply the witness of the thoughts. It is formless and changeless, unborn and undying, devoid of quality and yet absolutely intensely aware. In fact, it is awareness itself. It is boundless radiant presence.

As you become more and more intimate with that presence, you will clearly recognize that you are not the product of your thoughts. You will experience for yourself that you have never done anything wrong, that you have always been exactly where you needed to be, and that you have never been separate from your true nature.

Nothing exists which is not fully and completely divine. Everything is divine simply because it exists, because divinity is existence itself. The only seeming variable is the degree to which the individual is aware of this experience. This gives the illusion of growth and a path.

All that ultimately needs to be surrendered is control. This can happen in any moment and is a conscious choice. Instead of trying to remain in control of everything, give back control to Consciousness. Hand the steering wheel of your life back to God; she's a better driver than you.

Even in turning to offer the wheel of control over, you may see that you were never driving in the first place. The ego is like a little child in the passenger seat with a plastic wheel, and for a brief time it actually believes it is driving. Give it up.

Control is a deep habit, so to be free requires the willingness to persevere. To surrender control as quickly as possible, be willing to not take any of it seriously. As your awareness expands, you will see the structure of your ego. You will see the things that you believed to be true which have kept you separate forever. When you see these things, laugh at them.

From the outset, it is good to cultivate the ability to laugh at yourself. In order to be free you must master the mind, but a sense of humor is essential. It is a funny thing, and you can easily enter the search for Truth with the perspective of adventure and fun.

70. Why do I feel like I understand less as I explore more?

What a great place to be...know nothing and you gain everything. The mind wants to know and understand everything so that it can maintain control. What you know about consciousness means nothing in light of the direct experience of your true nature. Applying this is what it means to surrender. To take everything you think you know and lay it at the feet of the Divine. "I don't know anything, and I'm ready to come home."

A great Teacher once said, "Unless you are like little children you won't see the Kingdom of Heaven." Innocence is your natural state. Wonder is your natural state. Silence is your natural state. It is the simplest of things because it only requires you to let go.

It is important to realize that the mind cannot actually *know* anything. To know is not its job. The mind can only know *about* things. To know something, all understanding must be surrendered to the direct experience.

When I started to look for Truth, I felt like a baby. Everyone else had read so many things and done so many courses. I began to feel like I didn't have enough time in this life to catch up. Happily, the school of consciousness is unique in that you enter in University and graduate in Kindergarten!

The really amusing thing is that as you give up all that needless control, you can rest effortlessly in the source of all knowledge, all creativity. In that perfect, silent presence you are literally bathing in infinite, unbounded wisdom, and the desire to know anything disappears. You give up a little and gain a lot; you gain everything in fact.

So understand nothing, simply let it wash through you. It is the Silence that teaches, the Silence that heals, and the Silence that frees. Simply rest and let go of the need to understand, it doesn't apply here.

71. How does one develop and maintain a spiritual focus in ordinary life?

Developing a spiritual focus has already begun; otherwise you would not be here. You know that it is possible to have a different experience of life, and you are actively seeking it. Now it is a matter of making that your number one priority. No matter what your circumstances are, this is your life, the gift you have been given for the purpose of remembering who you are. Whether or not you use this life for that purpose is up to you.

Focus is only a matter of where you have your attention. For most people their attention is on the things that are always changing. Their attention is on the thoughts, the feelings, and the things they want to attain in order to feel more complete or more whole. It's not bad to have awareness of those things, but if that is the totality of your attention and focus then there is absolutely no chance of peace, none. Focusing on the changing is the very definition of *not* having a spiritual focus.

True spiritual focus is the recognition that, as you let go of identification with thought, there is peace, every time. Innocently allowing your attention to return to that presence of peace within is developing spiritual focus. It's like you are training your "spiritual focus" muscle.

Once you know how simple it is to let go of the mind in any situation and simply experience, then it is a matter of applying it, of doing it. There are a great many people who understand this as a concept and yet do not apply it in terms of their own experience. By taking some time during your day to use a practice of meditation, your focus naturally begins to shift.

For most people it is a gradual un-learning of the habits of a lifetime. Spiritual focus is all about developing a relationship with the silent presence of your own being, and making it the number one priority. The rest takes care of itself. It is a mistake to look to the conditions of your life as a marker of how you are doing. It is your *relationship* to the conditions of your life that brings peace, true peace.

The shifting of context from the mundane to the spiritual is a very inner thing, completely inner. Once you begin a spiritual path, the mind will try to divide your world into that which is spiritual and that which is not. The truth is, your whole life has always been spiritual; it is just that for most of it you have been ignorant of this fact.

Awakening is simply the recognition of that which has always been. There has only ever been God, and you have never been separate from that. There is a force for good in the universe that is in constant flow, and in any moment, you are either in alignment with it, or you are in denial of it.

Discovering for your self this force, and aligning more and more completely with it, *is* the spiritual path. The change is rapid and easy as long as you are willing to flow with it. Whatever tools or guidance you may draw to yourself, the focus has to be to become ever more surrendered to presence. This is how spiritual focus is developed and maintained.

72. Is it not selfish to put so much focus on oneself?

This is a common boundary when people are confronted with the choice to begin to move the awareness inward to peace. It would seem that to take time out to focus on that is a selfish thing, but the truth is quite opposite. Devoting some time to true peace is actually self*less*. By applying this principle to everyday life, you will clearly see it is true.

When you are stressed out, tired, overworked and in mental turmoil, truly, how effective are you in life? How much do you give to your family, your friends, your spouse or partner? More often than not, it is in these times when we are less likely than ever to be functional in virtually any relationship. It is also when we make the biggest mistakes at work or in business, when we are least healthy physically and emotionally.

Anyone who says they need stress to function efficiently is speaking without the direct experience of functioning any other way. I have talked to thousands of people about the possibility of living life in peace, and I have heard many, many of those people respond saying that they *need* their stress to function.

There is so much stress in modern life that most people function on adrenaline. The nervous system is taxed to the point of exhaustion, yet it is such a constant state that it seems natural. Even a seemingly happy person is, more often than not, functioning in the same way.

I worked in ski resorts for seven years in my twenties. I would watch as people came on a Friday night after a busy week at work, drive for hours and arrive late at night at the resort. Then they would get up early and organize the family for a day on the slopes, ski all day and then party into the small hours of the morning.

They would do the same thing the next day. At the end of the weekend, or week, they would then drive late into the night to return home, and be at the office the next morning more tired than when they left. It is a sad thing that even our supposed holiday time is driven by the need to do and do and do. Most people I have met in my life have no idea how to relax, no idea how to play.

Taking time to balance your inner life, through meditation, for instance, begins to bring back a right relationship to the mind and dissolve the stress that has accumulated in the nervous system. To some people, it may look selfish while you are taking a little time to meditate, but the possibility of having functional relationships, a productive work life and physical and mental well-being is greatly enhanced, simply by taking a little time for yourself.

This is the meaning of sayings such as, "Healer, heal thy self." In order to make a difference in the world, even our immediate world, it is necessary to take time to sort ourselves out first. The Ishayas have said forever that in order to heal the world it is necessary to heal ourselves. Gandhi said it perfectly, "Be the change you want to see in the world."

One of the most common things that transpires in the lives of those who have had a near death experience, where the body effectively dies for a time, is that there is a radical shift in life's priorities. Those for whom work came first and family second, almost always flip it on its head. Love becomes primary and all else second. It is not necessary to wait for this kind of event to start to make these kinds of choices. It is not necessary to stare death in the face in order to embrace life.

We have all had plentiful examples in our lives of how to put off the things that are the most important in our hearts. Most of the people who we have looked to have shown us, or even told us, that life is about living the way someone else thinks you should. Rare are the examples in the world of someone who is willing to put those things first, to live for the things that really matter and not to put them off or delay them. Truth and beauty and Love are endlessly available to everyone, and everyone deserves to be shown this and encouraged to live for those things. The world could surely do with a few more people that "selfish."

73. What is the most effective or correct way to meditate?

Meditation is experiencing each moment of life in awareness of peace. This is different than just feeling peaceful. It is literally living with an on-going awareness of the presence of God. Tools and practices of meditation should be about bringing this experience to conscious awareness.

When most people think of meditation, they think about someone sitting cross-legged, chanting mantras or other things. Meditation can actually be enjoyable. Not only that, but rather than trying to find twenty minutes of peace with the eyes closed, true meditation is focused more on the time between eyes closed sessions. Said another way, the benefits of the practice should be noticeable in life.

It all depends on what you want to get from meditation. For healing the body and achieving certain results in life, some visualization techniques are very effective. For calming the senses, certain breathing techniques can be effective. For revealing the true nature of the Self, you need to find something that will help you transcend the mind. Anything that focuses on sensory experiences, anything that puts the goal away in space and time, anything that reinforces the belief that you need to change or be fixed in order to become free will not work.

74. What teachings and techniques do you recommend?

I can recommend nothing more highly than the Bright Path teaching of Ascension. I don't say that because it is what I have given my life to, I have committed to this Teaching because everything I experience I owe to it. It is simple and powerful and never about waiting for another moment. It can be used eyes open or eyes closed and anyone can do it. It is mechanical, involves no belief, and so is completely safe. If you use it, it works. It gently and effortlessly allows the boundaries of judgment and belief to dissolve, in whatever time is right for you, gently and swiftly revealing your true nature.

Ascension requires no belief. If it is applied consistently, it is flawless. If you are not drawn to the this practice, then any teaching that brings your awareness into the presence of inner silence is going to be effective. In my experience however, techniques and teachings that have that inner silence as a consistent focus are few and far between. Even in the teachings that *do* have that as their focus, more often than not, the guidance provided is not always from a direct experience of having transcended the addiction to the mind.

If you want to wake up you need only be still now, and to surrender whatever your current experience is to God. Ascension allows you to do that effortlessly and continuously. It is the perfect mix of approach and withdrawal. It is simultaneously a letting go of the attachment to thought coupled with a direct focus of attention into the limitless field of awareness within which the thoughts arise.

Ascension uses a series of mechanical techniques, called Ascension Attitudes. What they do is allow you to simply and easily let go of whatever your limits are right now, immediately transcending the mind and taking the attention into the presence of peace. They meet you exactly where you are at and can be used eyes open or closed, and in this way they are unique.

CHAPTER 6

The Path of the Sages

In all traditions there has forever been an inner and an outer teaching. The outer teaching has been something that is palatable to the general population. Usually the outer teaching is one of making life a better experience, dealing in relationship to others and the world in a more effective way and finding relative peace. Many of the great Teachers of history veiled within this public ministry a hint of a deeper Truth that could be discerned by those who were spiritually ripe enough to hear it.

Jesus, for example, taught to the masses in parables and stories. Through this he was able to bring people to a better understanding of what their religion had been giving them for thousands of years. Yet within this, there were those who realized that a greater Truth was being offered, one that very clearly offered them the opportunity to become as he was. Of these a smaller number again were ready to surrender to him as Teacher and make the direct experience of the Kingdom of Heaven their first and only priority.

In the Ishaya Tradition this difference is spoken about as the Path of the Gods and the Path of the Sages. The Path of the Gods is one rooted in sensory betterment and personal comfort. Not a bad choice as it is still a slow spiritual advancement, and yet there comes a point in the evolution of every soul where this is simply not enough any more. It is at this point where the desire to know God as the Self absolutely takes over and nothing else will satisfy. Only losing oneself in the silent presence of All That Is will fulfill the purpose of life.

The Path of the Gods is also known as the path of comfort. This is a misleading term really. It seems to imply that the other path would be anything but comfortable. The greatest of ironies is that the path of comfort is the path that is littered with pain and suffering. There is no permanence in it, and no peace. No one ever wakes up walking that path. The other path, which is not labeled comfortable, is a path of instant peace and joy that increases forever.

These are actually not two paths; they are simply different expressions of spiritual maturity. There simply comes a point on every soul's journey that union with God without separation is seen as the only purpose and nothing else will satisfy. It is a moment of total humility and willingness to do whatever it takes. Once this choice is embraced, the universe responds to bring everything necessary for the end to be realized.

In Sanskrit, the ancient spiritual language of India, the world and universe are sometimes referred to as *Maya,* a dream. The Path of the Gods is about waking up within the dream, dreaming the best dream you can. The Path of the Sages is about waking up *from* it, and returning fully and permanently to union with God and the direct experience of the Kingdom of Heaven.

75. Is it true that all paths lead to God?

Yes...but the mind can twist this to make you complacent. It is true that all seemingly separated minds will return to awareness of their oneness with God, simply because separation is a trick of the mind. It never actually happened. Once it is recognized that waking up is possible, seeking a path with that as the goal is the wisest thing. To continue to walk a path that is rooted in anything other than awakening to your true nature is to consciously delay your freedom.

As your awareness and desire to be free expand, so you will discover more clearly the path of return, until the last vestiges of belief in separation evaporate. Humility and courage are required to surrender familiar beliefs and positions.

"When I was a child, I spoke as a child, but now that I am grown, I have put away childish things." (1 Corinthians 13.11) The goal of realization, once it is seen and desired, must remain at the forefront of your awareness. There are actually very few paths that end in that place: the bliss of freedom. Of those that do, some are swift and direct, some are not.

Ultimately, there are not two paths. As consciousness evolves, it goes through stages of ignorance falling away. Life goes from being seen as something to be survived and struggled through, then as something to be benignly experienced, eventually realizing that life is to be enjoyed, and finally realizing that life is to be transcended.

At some point along your journey you may be an angry or fearful person. Just through the experiences of life, one will eventually realize there must be more; there must be a different way to live. As you begin to search for that "more," you may become involved in a church or some other spiritual organization, replacing to some degree, the anger and fear to hope and faith. All is simply a manifestation of growth of awareness. Every level of consciousness has its own corresponding perception of truth.

As fear and survival are replaced by courage and faith as the operating principles of life, then courage and faith are replaced by love, and then love by silent presence, so the experiences of life evolve to serve further surrender into the heart of God. Even though these experiences seem to be different, it is one seamless evolution towards freedom, and so it is one path. The most important of shifts comes when living life for relative peace, for the illusion of personal comfort only, is no longer fulfilling. At this point, the attitude becomes, "I want to wake up, and I am willing to do whatever it takes."

It is the mind's proclivity to freeze frame eternity into little pieces and then label the pieces as worthy or unworthy, good or bad, that creates the seeming distinction between one path and another.

In truth, it is one continuous flow of remembering, and it never stops. The path appears to wind back and forth, going nowhere, until it gets straighter, but it is the ripeness of the individual that determines the directness of the journey.

Once you clearly see that you have always been exactly where you needed to be, you will also see that everyone is exactly where they need to be - automatically. To concentrate on your own journey is enough. Eventually, the only point of reference is the silent presence within.

Having said that, once you know that the path to freedom is to realize the Divine within, wasting time on frivolous things is to delay the goal. This is really your choice. To delay freedom unconsciously is one thing, but to delay it consciously is a tragedy.

76. Why is the path of awakening often likened to a razor's edge?

Eventually the choice between separation and freedom, between peace and your story, becomes so clear that there is no room to move. That is not to say that you couldn't move, or that you don't from time to time, but the return to peace becomes instant as soon as you notice you left it. The conscious choice for separation and limitation becomes completely unpalatable.

When the experience of the silence is so satisfying, and your ego's story is unattractive even to you, then you are on the razor's edge, right here in the presence now...unwilling to consciously leave it for anything. Welcome to life!

You can also term it the Path of the Sages. You have consciously made the choice that relative happiness will not alone satisfy any more. It is simply making the choice that awakening to your true nature is the purpose of your life. You have made the choice that there is not one position, not one limitation, not one false belief or opinion that you want to hold on to. As all are false, all must go in order to be free.

The surrender of these things is actually easy and joyful. The moment you choose to simply let go of a position you are holding, peace increases instantly and automatically. There is no need to wait for another moment. The feedback is immediate.

The mind will still kick and scream for a while. "Hey remember me? It's all well and good for you to find eternal peace, but what about all the problems out there?" The ego will serve it up the way you like it...but you just decide you don't need the calories anymore.

Even though the choice becomes clearer, and in that clarity, easier and more joyful, it also becomes more important. Once you have a clear, subjective experience of the presence of God, it becomes increasingly important to make that your number one priority, until it becomes the only thing.

It is always possible to choose again for separation and ego, but the greater the experience of the One, the greater the ramifications of turning one's back on it again. There are no down sides to freedom, but the down side of limitation is intensified after true awakening has begun.

Whatever your ego's favorite self-indulgence, it will be offered. All the Sages who have walked the path before have had this experience. Christ was shown that with the power he had accumulated, he could have anything of the world he wanted. This is symbolized by the devil (his ego) offering him the world if they joined forces once more. He refused, giving all glory to God.

Buddha was confronted with his "demons" while meditating, and again refused the temptations of each one. The mind, the ego, has only the power over us we willingly give to it. To surrender these things is easy once they are seen for what they are, nothing more than the desire of the small self to own that which rightfully belongs to God. The path of surrender has been modeled perfectly by those who passed through all of the ego's limitations. This willingness to surrender all thought, feeling and action to the will of God is what it means to be walking the razor's edge. The mantra is simple, "Thy will be done."

77. Why does this razor's edge seem the opposite of Rumi's saying, "There are a million ways to kneel and kiss the ground?"

Anyone can kneel and kiss the ground, but that won't wake you up. You can kiss the ground, a picture, icons, statues, people, and it may fill a little hole inside for a while, it may remind you of something more, and devotion in that sense is a beautiful thing.

To realize the Self, devotion needs to be turned inward, and ultimately surrendered. Devotion as a pathway will only get you so far. There will come a moment when the object of devotion, which is always separate, must be surrendered to the experience of pure awareness, no subject, no object...One thing.

There are a million pathways to the door, some fast, some slow, but only one entrance, and that entrance is surrender. That surrender can occur at any point on the journey, by the way. At some moment, you will see that the only place you can surrender to God is here, and the only time you can do it is now, and that will be true forever.

That is why the Ishayas say that there is truly only one Teaching. It is the teaching of what you are now, and the teaching of what you have always been and what you will always be. There is this moment that you are conscious and able to rest in your own true nature. Becoming more and more familiar with that takes on the appearance of a path. As your experience refines to the point where you consciously recognize your true nature as the presence of God, then it's over...or rather it has begun.

Then the dance becomes seeing that there are some things you are willing to leave the presence of God for, some things that still entice you. Seeing these habits, then choosing not to bite is the razor's edge.

How you get to this point is up to you, but this is the end of kissing the ground and the beginning of truly surrendering to God. This is the Path of the Sages. It is simple. It is joyful. It is straight, it is narrow and it is fast.

78. The razor's edge seems to imply that this path is difficult.

It may sound so, but it is not. The razor's edge is simply refining your focus to the point where you are unwilling to leave the experience of divine peace for anything. You begin to see all the things that you would willingly leave the presence of God for, and you just don't do it.

It can seem difficult if you say you want eternal peace, and yet still want to control the journey at the same time. It can seem difficult if you say you want to know God fully and yet still have things you want to get out if it for yourself. Once you have committed to awakening, the journey is learning the exquisite art of surrender to a higher will.

Again, the masters of the past have left clear instructions to allay the fear that this is a joyless process. "Seek first the Kingdom of Heaven and all else will be added unto you." Seek your freedom as the top priority and you get everything else too. Make waking up your priority and life will become smooth and rich and full, but put God first.

There is usually a period of in-ing and out-ing, but it doesn't take long for the payoff of separation to lose its attraction. To put it another way, if you can imagine that right now you are in the presence of God, how many things would you be willing to leave that experience for? The ego says, "Hi God, thanks for showing up, listen, hang around for a few minutes because I really want finish this thought stream I'm having about what an asshole my neighbor Bob is." It sounds funny, but consciously choosing for judgment over the Divine Presence becomes that absurd.

Freedom involves absolutely no effort and the reward is instant. The moment you just let go and rest into yourself, there is more peace than there was a moment before. If you allow yourself to consciously recognize that, and make it a priority, the experience of peace becomes far more tantalizing than all the things your mind will tell you are important. It does require willingness, and dedication, but no effort. It is simple and it is joyful, and anyone can do it. All that is required is the desire to be absolutely free, and the willingness to do it, no matter what. A little bit of effort and you're almost there, no effort at all…and you're there.

79. Isn't it true that there are countless paths available?

There are countless paths, it's true. What it is good to be aware of is that there are also countless destinations. If you know you want to remember your divinity, then the number of paths available to you is significantly reduced, because not many will bring you to that destination.

You can go to any train station, and there are countless trains, all as wonderful as each other. When you know your destination, however, the choices narrow. It doesn't take away from the beauty of the other trains; it simply makes your journey smooth, swift and clear.

Don't get me wrong, you can still choose any train you want to choose. You may choose the blue train because you really like blue, it feels so good to you and the seats look really comfortable, and that pretty lady got on even though you know the red train is going where you want to go. You have the choice, but don't blame anyone else if you end up somewhere else.

Waking up requires transcending the mind and cultivating a clear and ongoing awareness of inner silence. There is no fixing of the broken parts of you needed, nothing needs to be added to you, and what you seek is always, always present in it's fullness, not off in another time or place. No matter how attractive a path may seem to your mind, if it is about anything other than that, it will not lead to your true nature, it will not awaken you to your divinity, it will not reveal the Kingdom of Heaven.

80. What kind of commitment is required to realize the Divine within?

100 percent commitment, nothing else works. This is so because all of the things you currently believe to be more important have to be let go of. No spiritual seeker thinks that there are things more important to them than the presence of God, but that is the whole reason that enlightenment is not the constant experience of virtually anyone who has ever lived. The presence of God does not diminish ever, nor does it go anywhere, yet in each moment of perceived separation we *choose* that separation. It doesn't seem that separation is a choice and yet it is, and we make that choice in each and every moment.

In order to transcend separation completely, you must get to a place where you are willing to do whatever it takes to wake up. It is a radical shift in priorities, but without it there is no chance of awakening. Without that level of willingness and dedication, even on a spiritual path, the mind will at some point draw a line in the sand and say, "This is far enough." You have to be willing to surrender *all* positions, *all* attachments, *all* beliefs and *all* judgments.

The rarity of awakened beings is not because the goal is difficult; it is simply because this level of commitment is rare. The path is joyful and easy, but the mind believes there are things that are more important. When this level of commitment is talked about, you may feel a little pinch inside, a little nervous tension. This is an indication of places inside where there are things you have been unwilling to let go of, things you have made more important than your highest desire.

Once the priorities are reset to put awakening first, it is surprising sometimes how swiftly the universe organizes itself around you to support that. It is designed to function this way. You just have to maintain 100 percent commitment to the goal, to keep it as the first priority.

Once you have clearly discovered your true nature as consciousness aware, the game then becomes seeing and surrendering all of the things that you will actively leave that experience for. You could say that through alertness and humility you will identify your false idols, those things that are more attractive to you than your freedom. Once you have seen them, then you have your power back, and it doesn't take much time to break the habits of literally lifetimes. Most people do not want to see their cherished separate thoughts; there is a kind of embarrassment at being 'found out.'

There is no judgment from the Absolute about false beliefs. When you experience the unconditional love of the Presence within, the subtle and insidious idea of punishment for your sins, of punishment for turning your back on God, dissolves.

It makes it a lot easier if you can cultivate a spirit of adventure about the whole thing. The less seriously you can take it, the better. You really need a sense of humor about it because you are going to see the whole structure of your ego, which without a sense of humor can be rather awkward! It's actually hilarious. So commit to your freedom with every fiber of your being. Fifty percent committed won't do it. Ninety-nine percent committed won't do it. Only 100 percent commitment will get you home.

Like the Christian Gospels say, "Love the Lord your God with all your heart and all your mind and all your soul." It is an amazing thing too, because that commitment is continually expanding. In my experience, what it means to be 100 percent committed is a growing thing. I have always been as committed as I was able, and yet what was 100 percent a year ago, or a month ago or even a week ago would not be 100 percent now. It requires a constant re-commitment to Truth, and nothing brings greater joy.

81. I have heard of those who awakened suddenly and easily. Some didn't even adhere to any particular spiritual practice. It was like somewhere along the way the lights came on.

It has apparently happened like that for some. There are two potential problems though. The first is that you are only seeing the moment of their awakening, and not all other moments that led up to it. You are not taking into account all of the intense recognition of separation that led up to that moment of surrender. I have read of Eckhart Tolle's example, and it seems like for him, the internal suffering became so intense that complete surrender or death were the only options.

It is wise to be aware of two things: The first is that for everyone who has woken up, there was a moment that preceded it. Regardless of how the awakening occurred, let it be an inspiration to you to wake up too. The second thing is not to transpose someone else's experience onto your own. If someone appears to have awakened with no help whatsoever, do not let your mind turn that into an excuse to wait. Discover what creates the illusion of separation, and do what you can to learn to let it go.

The chances of awakening spontaneously are so slim that, if you really want to be free, you wouldn't leave it to that possibility. It's akin to needing money to get something you want, and waiting to win the lottery because it happened to somebody else. I will tell you that you have a greater chance by far of winning the lottery than spontaneously discovering your true nature in its fullness.

In truth, everyone wakes up in an instant; everything leading up to that moment is preparing you to let go. To some extent, you may need to hear a teaching in order to be inspired to be free. You may need to learn to meditate so you can see for yourself the false beliefs and positions. You will almost certainly need some guidance to recognize, and become familiar with, the perfect silence of your own consciousness.

All of it is kind of like standing on the highest diving board for the first time. Do you remember that feeling? "1-2-3...whoa wait a minute. OK, I'm ready...1-2-3...OK, OK, you go first and then me. 1-2-3...wait, I'll just go down a level, jump from there, and *then* come up here and do it." That's the spiritual path, the great cosmic diving board delay!

All that is required to wake up is to surrender all sense of an individual self to the Absolute. Unfortunately for most people, there is still enough investment in the individual self that this won't happen. Even if there *is* the intense desire to unite with God, there is not a clear enough experience of that presence to be able to surrender completely to it. Spiritual practice and guidance prepares one for the moment of complete surrender to the Divine. Little by little, there is a clearer experience of how the mind limits and confines you, and simultaneously, a growing experience of the presence of the infinite. Your mind cannot take you there. Your mind is the opposite of surrender.

82. What is renunciation?

By definition, renunciation is to give something up. In a spiritual sense, it is generally seen as the giving up or leaving of worldly life to focus on the spiritual. Unfortunately, this almost always sets into play a huge chasm of separation between that which is seen as spiritual, and that which is not. The belief that God exists only in certain things is a concept, and at some point must be transcended.

True renunciation is surrendering every thought, feeling and action to the will of God. The root of all pain and suffering is ownership, owning for yourself that which has nothing to do with you. This is *my* thought, *my* feeling, *my* life. You experience these things, and yet they appear spontaneously within the silent, limitless field of awareness we call God.

Maharishi Sadashiva Isham wrote, "What must one give up to realize the goal? Nothing. What must one be willing to give up? Everything." Nothing has to be given up except for our attachment to the mind; the belief that we create our thoughts, and that they have the power to tell us who and what we are.

When you decide that what you want is eternal peace, there will be wise and discerning choices that will obviously serve to achieve that. Yet, looking for all the places that you are broken and need to be fixed to be worthy of freedom, or where the world is broken and is unworthy of God, is actually counter productive.

As one evolves, certain things may fall by the wayside, but this is a natural *by-product* of evolving consciousness, not as a means to achieve it. It is always an expansive thing to leave behind something that no longer serves, whether that is an action, a desire, or a thought. Renounce the belief that you are the mind and body, and then freedom is easy.

83. Is renunciation the same as surrender?

Ideally, yes. Neither of them have anything to do with getting rid of physical things. True renunciation is renouncing the idea that you are the thinker of thoughts or the doer of actions. It is renouncing the belief that you are limited in any way. It is renouncing the belief that you are the body or the product of the thoughts in your head.

Surrender is really the same thing. It is allowing every thought, feeling and action to return to its source. Any limiting thought or experience that comes into your awareness, you just allow it to come, and allow it to go. It is not your job to own any of it, or figure any of it out.

Your natural state is to simply experience without judgment, in perfect innocence and wonder. Your natural state is a continuous, awe-filled experience of holding nothing.

If you are holding on to anything; any thought, any feeling, any past experience, you are blocking the good coming to you. Whatever you call it, renunciation or surrender, it is a state of seamlessly emptying your cup and allowing it to be filled again. It is the most magical way to live, the only way to really live, I would say.

84. Is it necessary to surrender everything to be free?

You don't need to surrender anything in terms of leaving physical things and experiences. It is necessary, however, to surrender all attachments, judgments and beliefs. While you attached to a particular thing, belief, position or outcome, then freedom is not possible.

To cling to the things of the past only keeps separation alive. It prevents the awareness becoming absorbed in the present moment.

It is hard to understand that in everything there is a gift, but it is true. Generally, when we appear to be losing something, we are so focused on what seems to be being taken away, that we do not see what is trying to be given to us.

One of the Hindu images of the Divine is called Narayana, the will of God. He is pictured with four arms. I have always loved that because if one hand appears to be taking something away, there are three other hands trying to give you something, but if you are so focused on what is going away, and how terrible that is, you will miss the gifts.

Being willing to surrender all attachments is not a test from the Divine to see if you deserve to be free; it is simply a truth. Attachment and freedom *cannot* co-exist. Investment in outcome and union with God *cannot* co-exist. Enjoying fully every experience while holding nothing at the same time is the doorway to freedom.

I was actually quite excited by the idea of surrendering everything. I didn't see it, but I was actually hoping that God would take away the things I didn't feel I deserved, or didn't know how to deal with. I was attached to *not* having some things!

If I had gotten rid of everything I judged as wrong, I would still have had the one thing that was keeping me limited, my judgments.

That's what we have to be willing to surrender. Surrender your attachments, surrender you beliefs, surrender your judgments and you will not only find eternal peace, but you will have the fullest of lives as well.

85. What does it mean to surrender attachments?

It is our attachments that keep us running around on the hamster wheel of the mind, delaying our peace seemingly forever. The things we are attached to are the things we believe we need to fulfill or attain before we can be free. Said another way, most people believe there are certain things that will make them happy, or more complete. The result of this is that there is an endless chase to accumulate material things to enhance the sense of self. The world has given us a false sense of success, and so life has become a race to live up to this external ideal for our sense of self-worth or lack thereof.

Once one begins the journey of Self-discovery, this same habit is almost always in play. We begin to try to fix all the seemingly broken areas of ourselves so that one-day, when we have completed the process, we will be free. This habit is the one thing that keeps us in separation and pain. We deal with or fix one area of ourselves only to find another thing to fix. What sense of achievement there is, is rooted in the mind's false belief that you are closer to the goal now, you are really making progress now, you are almost there now.

There are teachings that say, or have been interpreted to say, that we must identify and release all of our material gains. This leads to all kinds of craziness nobly labeled renunciation, where people will leave family, loved ones or entire cultures to go and hide away from what they perceive to be the blockages to realization. This is all dealing with the outside, and 99.9% of the time it is totally ineffective.

The attachment to the idea, "I am the body and mind," is the thing that needs to be surrendered. Life is not the problem. It is all about who and what you *perceive* yourself to be. You don't need to hide in a cave to realize your true nature. In fact, that is almost always counter-productive. As you surrender the attachment to the belief that you are the body and the mind, all other limiting beliefs become clear naturally, and are also easily surrendered.

86. What is the difference between the will of God and personal will power?

The difference is attachment to the outcome. If you are imposing your personal will on any situation you are attached to the outcome. Not only are you attached to the outcome, but also you are certainly also invested in *how* the outcome unfolds.

You can be moving towards something, some goal, and the road appears to be changing direction. If this brings stress and worry, fear and doubt, then you're invested in the outcome. Being willing to flow with the new direction and see what happens is being surrendered to a higher will.

There is a quote, "Lord, grant me the power to change the things I can, the serenity to accept the things I can't, and the wisdom to know the difference." This is surrender to a higher will.

Personal will is rooted in control, and control in that sense is an illusion. You have never had control. It is good to move towards the grandest vision of life you can, but recognizing the perfect unfolding of divinity allows you the freedom to live in the fullness of the present moment with an ongoing experience of perfect peace.

87. Surrender to God sounds very passive. Could you elaborate?

Surrender to God is anything but passive; it is an active choice. It requires attention to see the places where you unconsciously take ownership of that which is God's, and then gently give it back. Even though surrender is active, it is effortless. When you notice that you are invested in something, you will also notice the energy and effort required to do that, to maintain that investment of personal "me-ness." The letting go of that effort is surrender.

The ego will tell you that to surrender is weakness, but in fact, it is the doorway to strength beyond description. By surrendering everything that comes into your awareness to the presence of God, you align immediately with infinite power. There is nothing that boundless consciousness cannot achieve.

When you surrender your limited will to the limitless will of God, God is all that remains. Every impulse of creative potential that moves through you is in alignment with Divine Will. Without the investment in the limited ego self, you are an open vessel for the perfection of the Divine to unfold in its absolute purity.

88. Is it necessary to have a Teacher or to worship a Guru?

To worship, no, in fact this is counter-productive to the goal. The inner realization of the presence of true divinity can never come from worshipping the physical form, or experience of another. A true Teacher or Guru is a point of connection to the Absolute, and most importantly, a source of guidance for the journey into your *own* experience. If full awakening is your goal, having the guidance of one who has transcended the mind is invaluable. It is impossible to *think* your way to freedom; it is impossible for the mind to transcend itself. Having external guidance to surrender to is the surest way.

One of the things that can lead to pain instead of freedom, and be a distraction actually, is to begin a manic search for a True Teacher. There are many "Teachers" available who fulfill the outer requirements demanded by the mind, and yet often the essence is missing. This essence is the experience of Self-realization. To begin to search for a Teacher, the only reference point you will have is the mind's idea of what a Teacher will look like. One thing you can count on from the outset is that when it comes to spiritual advancement and freedom, the mind knows nothing.

Simply stay on your path, continue to seek freedom without compromise and eventually, when you are ready, the Teacher will appear. They will find you, or call you to them is a more accurate way to put it. If you are seeking freedom now, then I would tell you that the call has already happened, and by Grace you have heard. Stay alert and be open. If people could see themselves clearly, then they would see the Teacher in all things, but most people are not absolutely clear. Continue innocently and when you come face to face, you will know.

The Teacher is a seemingly outer manifestation of your own inner Presence. You will continue to move closer and closer to realization by committing to your path. Then, when you are in a place where you are ready to surrender everything to God, you will find yourself in the presence of one who can guide you home.

Don't let the search for a Teacher, or the rejection of its importance, become more of a priority than discovering your Self now. Simply continue relentlessly seeking Truth and all will happen with surprising ease.

When you do find the Teacher, surrender absolutely. To the best of your ability, which will continually expand by the way, do not compromise on that. Only by complete trust can freedom be won.

89. Why are there some teachings that say techniques and teachers are not necessary?

In one sense, after enlightenment, this may be so, yet virtually all realized beings have at some point surrendered to the guidance of an enlightened Teacher. There are very rare examples of those who have been born in extremely high states of consciousness such as Krishnamurti. There have even been those who have seemingly spontaneously awakened such as Ramana Maharshi, or Eckhart Tolle.

For those born enlightened, there is usually no concept of having been separate. There is no experience of having awakened from ignorance, and so direct guidance from them in transcending the mind is rare.

For those who awaken spontaneously, while separation is understood, there is no concept of a path to freedom from the mind. Their awakening "just happened." The guidance can be limited and even frustrating to the sincere student. Hearing about the difference between living in separation and living in union is inspiring, but being given a way to apply it in life and experience it for your self is everything.

Being in the presence of such beings is, in and of itself, immensely valuable, yet progress can seem slow. Finding one who has transcended duality and has a path to offer is rare, and more valuable than gold. The experience of enlightenment is so statistically rare that while it may be a possibility to wake up without guidance, you have a better chance of being struck by lightening in a rubber box at the bottom of the ocean.

These statements about not needing guidance may be meant in a spirit of truth, but they are usually interpreted very conveniently by the mind. For the seeker, the idea that a Teacher is not necessary very quickly becomes an excuse not to let go of control.

The mind would love to think it could figure out enlightenment. This is not possible. When a soul is ready, the Absolute will manifest in the form of a Teacher, or Teaching, or both, to guide them beyond the mind and into the heart of God.

This guidance comes in many forms over the course of the spiritual journey. First, it may be as an inspiring book or as a teaching of Truth. Then it may appear as a technique of meditation and so on. As each step is embraced and applied, the universe responds to the increasing level of commitment to freedom, and eventually appears as the awakened Teacher. If enlightenment is the highest desire, then yes, a Teacher is almost always required.

Even beyond being required, I would say it is actually inevitable. Once the desire for true freedom has begun to take root in consciousness, it will not be defeated. At any point in time, it may seem like one is on one path or another, but in truth it is all a ripening. There will come a moment when one has evolved to a level of ripeness and willingness that the Teacher, the inner force of evolution, will manifest on the outside. This impels growth at an infinitely greater pace, simply by having something seemingly external to surrender to.

This is purely by Grace. It is always possible *not* to surrender to that, by rationalizing it all, by going backwards into the mind to all the things we have heard or read about why one actually does not *need* a Teacher. It is easy to say that one is willing to do whatever it takes to wake up, but when you bump up against your positions, judgments and desire to control your own awakening, that's when "the rubber hits the road" so to speak.

The Teacher is a compassionate manifestation of your own inner Self, your true Self. It is completely beyond space and time and so has infinite patience. It will wait forever for you to be ready to come home. Just as to walk, it is inevitable one has legs, so to reach enlightenment, a Teacher or guide is also inevitable.

90. I have heard about gurus in India who can bestow enlightenment through touch. That seems a lot easier than this.

You have the common ailment of wanting someone else to do this for you. I hate to be the bringer of bad news, but it won't work like that.

You can definitely get some experiences from those who know. The presence of an enlightened being will automatically expand your experience, but realization of your true nature is *your* choice, and it will always be that.

I met a man once in Australia, who spent years with a famous swami in India. He was making a movie about it actually. This swami gave *shakti pat*, enlightenment by touch. This man told me most people only ever received *shakti pat* once or twice, but he quite proudly told me he had received it 167 times.

I was amazed, not that he had received it 167 times, but that even after that he couldn't stay there, he couldn't just remain in the Presence. The mind was opened to its true nature, yet he chose to leave it. He honestly believes that his guru gave him the experience, and that he has no choice about whether or not he returns. We never want to see the simplicity of what waking up actually is. We yearn for someone to do it for us, or for some magic pill. We want anything but to apply a teaching for ourselves and follow in the footsteps of the sages.

This is very convenient from an ego perspective, and absolutely not true. Identification with the mind got you into this mess, and the way out is by undoing your identification with the mind. You need to see, to actually see the dance you do with your mind, and the things that you believe to be true which are not, and to give them up.

You need to wake up. You are more than you have even begun to dream. You actually know that intellectually, but not as an experience. Don't die this close to what you want. It is closer than your next breath.

91. Why are there enlightened teachers who teach a hard path?

All of the greatest teachers have said that you are already That which you seek, that the Kingdom Heaven is within and at hand, meaning it is now. Enlightenment is the direct recognition of the inherent divinity of all things, exactly as they are. Teachings of penance for bad behavior, or rigorous practices to appease God are of no value, and are not a direct expression of higher truth.

For most teachers, the pathway they walk is the pathway they teach. The moment of awakening is by Grace alone, yet there appears to have been a path that got you there. If there has been struggle on the path, perhaps it will be taught as part of the journey.

It is far more likely in most cases that what appears to be enlightenment in the teacher is not so. External appearance is not the inner experience.

Just because you wear a white coat, drive a Mercedes and play golf on Wednesday afternoon doesn't make you a doctor.

The common denominator of the truly Self-realized, regardless of the path, is the all encompassing, eternal radiance of the presence of God, and the absolute simplicity of realizing it for your self.

More importantly than wondering why some teachers teach a hard path, which way do you want it to unfold for you? Do you want to suffer to be free? That may seem a silly question, but there are those, and many by the way, who believe they have to suffer to be free.

Many of us believe that, if I just suffer enough, just experience enough anguish, that God will have mercy and lift me up. It can go like that if you want it to, if you believe enough that this is how it has to be. This level of suffering for God is common in the experiences of the early Christian Mystics; the agony and the ecstasy, the dark night of the soul. Most of them didn't have another point of reference, another example of a simple, joyful path. They wanted the experience, the direct experience of God, but everything they could find to tell them how to get it was dripping with anguish... and it can be a self-fulfilling prophecy. Happily, this doesn't make it true. At the very least, it doesn't make it necessary.

Even though most of the world's spiritual literature says it has to be like this, the opportunity also exists to make it easy, graceful and joyful...but the choice is yours. Most people never get to hear this, but by grace you have. Now you have a different choice. The Ishayas have always taught an easy, joyful path. All the greatest teachers, the most realized beings have always taught the utter simplicity of the choice. If it was necessary to walk through hell to attain heaven, who would ever want to begin the journey?

Humans have conditioned themselves to believe that anything worthwhile must require great effort and sacrifice. Separation itself *is* effort and sacrifice. The path of return is surrendering those beliefs, and it is effortless and joyful. After all, your true nature is Bliss.

92. Is it necessary to retreat from ordinary life?

No. The idea that there is a spiritual life and an ordinary life is an idea only. There may be times when you feel to go on a retreat to meditate or get centered. But if the boundary exists between two things then eventually you will have to see it and let it go.

There has only ever been a spiritual life. You have always been creating your experiences from the perspective of the absolute. As I said, taking time to get some perspective is good, but you can have it all. Everything you experience, all of your friends and family, the air you breathe and the clothes you wear are all one thing.

There is only one infinite ocean of consciousness and you are that, always. Learn to take your attention off the things, the content, and experience the infinite, silent field within which they appear. This is the door, this is the way, and this is the key.

Running away from the world in a traditional sense is not necessary. In fact, the movement to do so is more often than not rooted in the judgment that there are certain places where God is not.

It's beautiful that it is in the Western world right now that the true Teaching is surfacing, the place where materialism has been lived to the extreme. Whatever your life is, it is meant to be lived with an ongoing awareness of its source, living fully *in* the world, yet not *of* it. Your natural state is to live a rich and full life, free from fear and judgment, with a continual awareness of your immortal self.

C H A P T E R   7

Experiences Along the Way

One of the reasons why guidance is so important along the spiritual path is that all manner of experiences present themselves, not all of which have the immediate value of moving one closer to Union.

Indeed, some of the most sought after experiences by spiritual aspirants are the ones that, in light of the ultimate goal, have little or no value. The mind is always enticed by the spectacular, yet freedom is the most simple and normal of experiences.

The desire to perform miracles, see lights, move the world by the power of thought, create vast mansions out of thin air, all of these things are distractions. For those without guidance, these things would seem like signposts of real spiritual evolution. They may or may not occur as consciousness evolves, but in and of themselves they do not mark the way. These powers can be developed by practices which focus on them, yet the practitioners, often, are no closer to Self realization. Wondrous powers do not necessarily speak to any degree of the realization of a particular being.

There is a great story from India about a man who was invited to dine with a King. Along the way to the palace on the eve of the feast, he found the streets lined with performers for the celebrations. All along the road were fantastic magic acts, and jugglers, storytellers and minstrels. His travelling companions would ask him why he did not stop to enjoy the shows.

"I am to dine with the King," he replied, "I don't want to offend him by being late."

And so he went on. Upon arrival at the royal court he was welcomed, and took his place of honor beside the King. Through the window he could see the faces of his friends in the crowds outside the palace. After a wonderful and elaborate feast, the King clapped his hands, and all of the minstrels who were performing in the streets entered and performed especially for them.

This is an illustrated version of Christ's saying, "Seek first the Kingdom and all else shall be added unto you." When you know what you want is to be free, to have permanent unshakeable inner peace, then making that your first priority is the only way home. All of the wonder and unfolding magic of consciousness happens as a by-product of that focus, yet it is not an indication of how far you have progressed.

On the road to enlightenment, stillness is the only reliable spiritual experience.

93. How do I know if what I am hearing is the voice of God or of the ego?

If you're hearing voices, there is a good chance that it is ego directing you. The voice of God is silent and still. It manifests as an inner knowingness, a spontaneous silent knowingness in consciousness.

So many people in this world are being run by voices in their head, in fact almost everyone, and a voice that tells you it is God's voice is a pretty enticing thing. Listen to God's voice like it is silent. Listen for it attentively. In that silence, all voices, all thoughts, all form dissolves.

The manifestations and voices that we attribute to the Divine can often be anything but. I heard a story of a guy in the United States who had a huge marijuana plantation in his back yard. His sister went to his house for a visit and was shocked by this because he had always been a strong Christian. She asked him why he had it. He said that he had a clear vision where Jesus had visited him one day and told him, "Don't worry my son, there is weed in my garden too." He considered that a green light to get as stoned as he liked on home grown pot!

There are countless stories of people doing quite horrendous things because, "God told me to."

There is no voice that is Gods; there is no voice that is yours. In this journey to freedom, Silence is literally golden.

94. Sometimes I notice that I am moving into a very deep stillness, and instantly there is this fear that jerks me back to separation. How do I stop that and just let go?

This is actually quite a common experience, and not a bad thing, really. It can create a judgment though. You can begin to judge yourself for leaving the one thing you want. You find yourself at the doorway to freedom and then pull away out of fear.

Don't see it as a problem. Simply continue on the path and eventually the fear will dissolve. It is not too dissimilar to a common experience people have when falling asleep.

Did you ever go to bed really tired, and then from out of nowhere you find yourself falling down a dream staircase and jerking violently back to normality? All that happens is that a deep level of the mind recognizes the depth of rest you are moving into, and scrambles to keep itself in play. The same thing happens as you are getting closer to letting go of the limited, small self. There is enough of the ego left intact to notice the infinite field of consciousness that is being presented. Like a cat sliding down a tin roof, it scrambles for a grip, clawing at existence.

The worst thing you can do is judge yourself for it. Rather than that, appreciate the fact that you have touched that level of awareness. By allowing yourself to recognize the silence within, and to get familiar with that, the fear naturally dissolves. You are beginning to discover, and will continue to discover, the silent presence that is beyond the mind. The more familiar you become with that presence, the idea that you don't exist there, or that there is something to fear, goes away.

You have not missed the opportunity to wake up, and you will be there again and again. You are moving closer to the readiness to make the ultimate surrender, to let go of the mind for once and for all. You have missed nothing.

95. I meditate for peace and tranquility, but all I experience is chaotic thoughts and random emotions. Am I doing something wrong?

No. This is the most common reason why people either stop meditating, or never even start. The idea that you have to stop your mind to be successful is simply not true. Neither is the belief that if thoughts enter your awareness that you are somehow meditating incorrectly.

Meditation, at least if it is of any value, is not about whether or not you have thoughts, but it is very much about whether or not you are *identified* with the thoughts. As you learn to watch the mind you will begin to discover the presence of peace that existed always. As you become more familiar with that peace and consciously rest your attention there, whether there are thoughts or not becomes irrelevant.

Language is always somewhat limiting. Stillness has nothing to do with an absence of movement. Silence has nothing to do with an absence of noise. These ideas are simply an attempt by the mind to get you to believe you are failing. In this endeavor to wake up you will not, and cannot fail.

In meditation, the chaotic energy of the mind begins to still. Simply by watching the movement, the energy begins to still and the mind moves quickly into rest. It is common knowledge these days that the mind and body are connected. What affects the mind affects the body and vice versa. As the mind rests, the body rests also, so meditation brings about immediate and very deep rest physically.

As the body rests in meditation, it begins to release impressions and stresses that have accumulated over the life span. This release of tension, stress and impressions causes the body to go into activity called healing. Due to the connection between the mind and body, this healing activity is mirrored in the mind as thought.

Said another way, the thoughts that come during meditation are a direct result of healing. The meditations you have had with the most thoughts, even though probably annoying to your mind, may have been the most healing experiences you have had. Let the thoughts come. As the nervous system clears, the experience of peace and stillness will be more permanent and on going, so let the body heal, let the thoughts come.

96.

With my meditation practice it seems like nothing at all is happening. I feel nothing, no peace or love. There is no difference in the state of my mind. It basically thinks the same things that it always has.

Of course it does, and so what? The mind is the ultimate babbling idiot. It just goes on and on and on, and not much about the content ever changes. It judges you, condemns you, praises you, encourages you, and then does the same thing with the world around you.

If it runs out of thoughts to think it just kind of sits there, humming to it's self. Have you ever noticed that? From out of nowhere a song starts up in your head, and more often than not it isn't even one you particularly like...your mind has terrible taste in music!

But something is changing for you, because you said, "It thinks the same thoughts it always has," so you are aware of your mind as an object to some degree. The current block for you is that your mind has an idea of what peace or love is, based on a transitory feeling. The thought comes up, "Nothing is happening, I don't feel any love," which is not *you* thinking by the way, but you recognize the voice as you and say to it, "You know what, you're right." You get involved in a dialogue with your mind about an experience, of which it can know nothing.

Immediately prior to the "I'm not experiencing any peace" thought, you were actually bathing in infinite peace, but then you follow a commentating thought, leave the experience of peace, and immerse yourself in the "nothing is happening" fantasy.

Here is the great mantra to free yourself from the commentating mind; So What? Whatever you notice the commentating voice say, say "So what?" in return.

True peace is not a feeling. True love is not a feeling. It is a state of being, an infinite field. Don't look for it because from the mind you have no idea what you are looking for. Simply open to it and do not take any direction at all from the thoughts in your head, your mind knows nothing of any value about true peace or love.

97. No matter what I do, I still feel lost and directionless.

Which direction are you looking to go? This is actually a common experience, and as consciousness continues to shift here on Earth, it is only going to become more common. There is a subtle knowingness that there is more to life, but because of the lifelong habit of looking to the outside world for a sense of purpose, coupled with the mind's propensity to try and control the outcome of everything, we don't see clearly what that purpose is all about.

You look at the conditions of your life and think that everything is supposed to be different, that there is something wrong with it all. The truth is, you have always been exactly where you need to be, and this will always be true.

There is a belief that if I could just see clearly which direction I should be going, then I could take the necessary steps to get there. This is all well and good, but it is not really possible to see anything clearly while we are still identified with the mind.

There is another way to go about it all. This way is through surrender to inner peace. As you learn to surrender to the silence within, you become open to the perfect unfolding of the purpose of your life. The sense of having no direction disappears, because you are no longer looking to the outside for your fulfilment.

The highest purpose of your life is to remember who you are, to return to a living awareness of your divinity. As you move towards that realization whole-heartedly, what you need to do in terms of your physical life becomes crystal clear.

This surrender is not passive at all, quite the opposite actually. Life becomes incredibly vibrant and alive. As you discover the reality of the perfect silence and peace within you, any concept that you could make a wrong decision disappears and you are free to actively engage the choices that are presented moment-to-moment. Everything is experienced with a conscious awareness of infinite presence.

I had the same experience of feeling directionless. In my twenties I was working in restaurants and bars, and yet had done a lot to wake up also, at least I had done the best I could with what I had found at the time. On that journey I had become a Reiki teacher and a massage therapist, amongst other things. I knew there was a purpose to my life, and the work I was doing didn't seem to me to reflect that purpose. Obviously I needed to change it. I quit my job and began teaching Reiki and doing massage.

I forced everything to support that choice, but all that happened was I went into debt. And then I found Ascension and the Ishayas. Instantly I knew this was my path, that this teaching held the key to me waking up. I knew I had to go and study with the Ishayas for as long as it took, but I was in debt from trying to force the hand of God.

I had an altar set up in my apartment where I would meditate every day. On it were images of various sages. I sat in front of my altar one day and burst into tears. I cried out, "I'm so sorry for trying to control everything. I want to surrender, please help me."

I'm not kidding, within five seconds the phone rang. It was my old boss from the restaurant who asked if I could come back and work again. They would pay me more money and give me the hours I wanted.

Within a short time I was able to clear the debt, and through some other magical circumstances, found myself with the Ishayas within a few months.

You see, once you get out of the way, the universe can move in the most amazing ways to bring your life to its fulfilment. While you are in the way and trying to control everything and figure it out, this cannot happen because you can't see the gifts that are being presented.

If you want to find direction and purpose, realize that your purpose is to wake up. When you know that, the direction is clear: inward. From there, your life is freed up to become what it was always intended to become, and that does not look any one particular way. Your job is to give up control and return your attention to presence.

98. How do I deal with intense emotions, thoughts, feelings and energy?

Take the label off. Emotion is, as is commonly taught these days, simply energy in motion. It is energy moving through your nervous system, but out of habit we learn to try and control it. The mind notices it and immediately wants to label it, based on past experiences. The energy moves and the mind says, "Oh no, here comes the sadness/anger/depression again." Then, after labeling it, we try to control it.

The second thing the mind does is attribute a cause to it. "Now I am angry, and it's your fault!" Not only have we tried to control the movement of energy at this point, but also we are off chasing a story about what caused it in the first place.

Simply relax and see if you can let the energy move without a label on it. Just let it be there. You may find that what at first appeared to be anger is something other.

For my whole life, there were times when I would experience an immense fear. It was usually at night, and more often than not, when I was alone. It was so intense that I would quite literally freeze in the bed, unable to move. There was not one thing that seemed to cause it, but the energy would begin to rise within me and within minutes I would be frozen in fear.

One night, the fear began to come on. As it was building, I noticed how much I was trying to control it. A part of me believed that it was so big, so intense that it would kill me if I let go. This particular night, I realized I couldn't fight it any more. I gave up, and if it was going to kill me, then so be it.

In that moment of surrender something magical happened. The energy was still there, but it was no longer experienced as fear. All the labels and the stories around it disappeared, and what was left was intense peace. All of the associations with the history of the fear in my life were dropped, and I was free of it.

If you have a familiar emotional energy in your life, play with not labeling it. Watch for the tendency to indentify and associate the energy with past moments, and play with letting those histories drop away. It takes a little practice, but it is so worth it. You may just discover that all negative emotions are simply bliss mislabeled.

99. I can't stop thinking. My mind is driving me crazy.

No. Your mind is constantly thinking. What is driving you crazy is the belief that you are the thinker. If you absolutely knew that none of the thoughts in your head were yours, then you would have no problem with any of them. The problem arises when you see the thoughts and then believe yourself to be the thinker. You are not.

Most people believe that they have control over their thoughts, that they in some way create them. If you did indeed have control over your thoughts, then you would most certainly create a much more pleasant mind than you have.

With only a little investigation you can see that thought arises out of the field of awareness itself. If you do not engage the thought and run with it, it subsides quite quickly back into the same field.

Try this for a day. Who is your closest friend? For a whole day imagine every thought in your head is coming from them. Who else is close to you?

So, all day today, every thought is coming from your friend and going to your wife. It is not your job to do anything with the thoughts, or interact with them in any way; you simply allow them to pass through your awareness from one point to the other.

Play with it. See how your relationship to the mind changes when you remember to do this.

Your job is to allow everything that enters your awareness to return, unhindered, to its source. Like clouds moving across the sky, just relax and allow the clouds of thought to move gently through the infinite sky-like field of your own conscious awareness.

100. When will I be free from painful emotions?

You will take a great step towards freedom when you no longer want to change your experience. This doesn't mean that you are going to try and *enjoy* what you see as negative, because that maintains the label and the story associated with it, and so keeps the experience locked in its current form.

Begin by not resisting the energy of it. Try not to label the energy and just let it be there. When you are no longer labeling the energy itself, then you can see the thoughts around it, and let them go. In order to resist the emotion, you have to identify it as something you don't want, and then engage the story about it, your personal history with it. "I remember this energy, and it's not good."

It is quite amazing actually, because the story prevents you from experiencing the purity of the energy as it is. The thoughts are the way you remember the energy being before, and so when you are locked in them, there is no possibility of being present with the energy as it is, brand new. It may not be what your mind *believes* it to be.

The painfulness is never in the energy itself, it is always in the thoughts around the energy, and the resistance they bring. You will see. In surrendering to the emotion as it is now, dropping the label and the story, there is simply energy. It is not longer called sadness or pain or whatever, it is simply energy, and no longer negative.

This is a step-by-step thing, but if you give it a chance when you can, the difference in your subjective experience will be clear, and that will be your motivation to continue.

101. What is the clear recognition of the presence of God like?

The presence of God is Still. It is a Silent Presence, and it is complete and whole. When resting in That, there is no concept of being broken, no concept of being better than, or more full than anyone else. There is silent awe and wonder at the eternity of the Self.

The mind can imitate all manner of experience. It can imitate intensity or colored lights. It can imitate ecstasy and such, but it can never imitate silence. The mind cannot imitate stillness, for the nature of the mind is movement. When there is stillness, there is no mind, at least no identification with it. This is why the only reliable spiritual experience is silence.

Through the development of the ability to witness the mind objectively, the gentle presence of your true nature begins to be revealed. Firstly, it appears as fleeting glimpses, then as extended moments, and then as a permanent, ongoing experience.

Having guidance is critical because we are simply not used to experiencing that which is beyond qualities. There are many spiritual paths and practices that cultivate the ability to watch the mind, but few direct the awareness into the recognition of that which is watching.

Beyond the chatter and movement of the mind is a constant, still, silent witnessing presence. It is all encompassing and eternal. It is changeless and formless. It does not love, it is Love itself. It is not peaceful, it is Peace itself. It is the root of all things, and nothing exists separate from it. It is the presence of God, and it is also the real you.

102. Why do I get bored and easily distracted when I'm meditating?

Because of a thought, that's it. A thought was moving quite happily through your awareness saying, "This is boring," and you looked back at your experience and talked to the voice, saying, "why, yes it is."

That commentating voice that decided the experience is boring never actually *was* in the experience you were really having; that's not possible. It was commentating about the way the experience was *just a moment before.*

In looking back at how the experience was a moment ago, you leave the present, which is perpetually rich and full, and where the concept of boredom does not even exist. Within the richness and fullness of the present, the mind says, "Boring." Then you engage in analyzing whether it *was* indeed boring or not, and basically just start talking to the voice in your head.

In all of it you have moved completely out of the present moment, left the peace, stillness and silent joy that you want, and engaged a dialogue about a moment which has gone, and so can be nothing but flat.

All of the commentary about the experience, even positive commentary, is about any other moment than now. Your mind, no matter how well intentioned, cannot possibly comment, or add to, your present experience. *Every* thought is about the past or the future, *never* about now.

So, explore treating the "it's boring" thought as just another thought. See what happens if you don't engage it and gently let it go.

The annoying phenomenon of being distracted is simply born by still being attracted to movement. Don't take it too seriously, but see what happens if you play with letting these thoughts be seen as just thoughts. As you explore, the silent beauty of the present becomes more attractive to your awareness than a voice in your head.

Little by little and step by step; don't expect to master this in a moment. Playfully watch and discover for yourself. That voice in your head is *not* you. You are what is *aware* of the voice. See it for what it is, let it go on its way, and discover peace.

103. I find when I smoke marijuana it enhances my spiritual experience. Is that ok?

Smoking marijuana can seem like it enhances your spiritual experience, but what it's actually enhancing is the experience of your senses. If you smoke, that's not a bad thing and not a good thing, but when you put it in context, then you can make choices.

Anything that artificially enhances your senses is, on some level, causing stress to your nervous system. Meditation is about releasing stress from your nervous system so you can be free. It's like saying you want an empty bathtub, and then pouring water into it because you enjoy the sound of the splashing.

There are a couple of drawbacks to using drugs to experience altered states of consciousness. One is that once the drug wears off, that state of awareness also wears off. In order to experience the heightened state again, you need to take the drug. Far from being an ongoing experience of your true nature, you are merely experiencing yet another, transitory sensory experience, one that you are dependant on an outside source to obtain. It may be a nicer, more ungrounded state of being than your everyday life, but it is limited and externally induced.

The thing about using drugs is that whatever you experience is sensory. The high is always based on how you are feeling, what the world looks like, how sounds are different. This is not even close to the glory of true freedom. It is just a beautiful limitation.

There aren't any rules, but if you know what you want, then you can make your choices accordingly. In the same way you do not need anyone else's approval to be whole, or anyone else's permission to be free, you do not need any external substance to realize your immortality, in fact no external substance is capable of giving you that.

Many people who enjoy smoking and doing drugs react badly to a statement like that. "Shamans do it, it's a valid spiritual path."

Well, firstly, you're not a Shaman. Secondly, Shamans use substances to induce visions; sensory, exalted visions...for a purpose. It isn't that using drugs can't be a step on the path. I, and many people I know, used drugs because it was the only way we knew to experience something other than the daily, mundane physical world. There comes a point, however, where the drugs no longer serve, and so if you are smart, you stop and do it a different way.

104. What is meant by the "Dark night of the soul?"

This statement is referring to the anguish and suffering that many who have walked the path to inner realization have, historically, described. It is a term that is prominent among the Christian mystics. Most have approached this journey without guidance of any quality, and it is this experience of the "dark night of the soul" that shows the value of guidance very clearly.

It is common for the subtle levels of the mind to confuse *feelings* of divinity and love with the absolute presence of God. While these feelings emanate *from* the Presence, they are not the Presence itself.

All feelings, no matter how sublime and beautiful, will change, for they exist in the realm of the changing. If one experiences these feelings, sometimes for extended periods, and believes that this is the presence of God, what happens when the feeling goes away? God goes away. Having tasted it, this is anguish for the seeker. God appears to become impermanent, and the mind goes into guilt and fear.

These experiences have been so well documented that there is even a common belief that they are necessary. It becomes almost heroic to suffer for God. The ego feels like it is really getting close to the goal the more intense the suffering becomes. This whole thing sets up a tragic split in the mind: The desire to be free from suffering, and the need to suffer for freedom.

All of this can be avoided with the guidance of a realized being, one who has gone beyond suffering and clearly experiences the underlying reality of all that is. As the experiences along the way are shared with the Teacher, he or she can guide the student easily beyond the transient experiences of the mind into the unchanging reality of the One.

Beyond all movement, there is an experience of unmoving silence, perfectly stable and eternal. Alone and without the guidance of one who knows, it is virtually impossible to discover that presence for what it is, simply because of the mind's endless habit of seeking out, and identifying with, feeling and movement. It is literally impossible for the mind to go beyond itself.

Christ told his students, "I have come to bring you something which cannot be touched by the hand, and cannot be seen by the mind. I have come to bring you something which has not even arisen in the heart of man." He was speaking of something that transcends all sensory levels of experiencing, including feelings, yet it can be realized directly and simply.

It is not necessary to suffer at all to return to Oneness with God. There is nothing for which you need to atone in order to be forgiven. In the moment of realization, there is a complete knowingness that you, and consequently all of humanity, have never done anything wrong. This is radical for a world hinged on guilt and punishment, and yet it is Absolute truth.

The Kingdom of Heaven never leaves us. God never leaves us. Through our belief that we are never quite enough now, *we* leave *it*, and we do so continuously.

For those who associate the Absolute with the changing realm of feelings, once those feelings subside, as they surely will, it will seem as if God has subsided also. The belief that they are somehow not enough for God is reinforced, and wracking guilt ensues. You can avoid this mistake; it is not necessary.

Many are those who would walk through Hell to unite with God, only because they have been shown no other way. Few are those who would walk through Heaven. The path is yours to choose.

CHAPTER 8

The Ones That Got Away

105. How can I find the "perfect partner?"

The search for the perfect partner is really the search for the true beloved within. We are searching to unite with the part of ourselves that we feel is missing. *or searching for commoness to strengthen + enlighten us.*

Virtually nowhere in the world are we taught to discover that experience within ourselves first. Every movie, every song on the radio, almost every single person we would know or meet, is showing us that we need someone else to complete us, to make us whole, as well as reinforcing the idea that the path to discovering that magical "other" is a path of anguish and being let down.

The desire for a fulfilling relationship is not a bad thing; in fact you deserve it. Any relationship that you have, however, will always be less than its full potential while you are still separate from the source of true love.

The experience of love will always be conditional while there is a sense of needing any kind of validation from the other person. Initially, upon meeting the person we think might be "the one," everything about that relationship appears to be better than we could have dreamed. Then, once our own patterns of low self-worth and judgment kick in, we project those things onto the other person, and the shine quickly comes off the relationship.

In order to find an ideal partner, you must become that. The only way to become that is to release all of the judgments and self-criticisms that play in your mind. You are lacking nothing and you do not need anyone else to complete you. While you feel like you need someone to complete you, the relationship you seek so much will elude you.

The true beloved is your own consciousness. The true beloved is your own divinity. As you unite with that, more often than not, it manifests in the outside world too. The best part is, whether it does or does not show up in life as an ideal partner, it won't matter any more because you will be whole and complete already with an infinite love as your state of being.

As you begin the journey into your own divinity, you are beginning the ultimate romance. You are discovering your own perfection and beauty. You are falling in love with the source of every experience. It will never leave you; in fact it *has never* left you. It will never judge you, and holds you forever in your perfection. It does not only love, but it *is* love. It is your own radiant presence that has been waiting for the perfect partner, and that partner is you.

106. What is Karma?

Karma is a Sanskrit word referring to the apparent universal law of cause and effect. While one lives in identification with the mind and ego, every thought feeling and action that ripples out into creation will eventually return to its source bearing fruits. These may be pleasant or not.

Karma is seen as a purely Eastern idea, but it has always been a big part of all spiritual traditions. This includes the early Christian teachings. The Councils at Nicea and Ephesus, which formulated what teaching would actually reach the public, removed all the overt references to karma. The idea of karma infers that you are returning to union with God, not a perpetual sinner. "As you sow, so shall you reap." This is karma.

Even in places where karma is spoken of, it is usually taught as an Eastern version of original sin. It is true that action has reaction, but the teaching of karma, as is commonly understood, creates the belief that you cannot be free now, that you are not worthy of your birthright now. It is a teaching of all the reasons why you don't deserve to come home now.

There is no other time to do it. There may be residual beliefs in the mind that are so strong that you won't undo them immediately, and this is true karma. Identifying with these beliefs will continue to bring about the same results, until the identification with them is surrendered. What you are learning to surrender and move beyond is identification with the ego, and in a very real sense, ego and karma are the same thing. As you undo the ego, you undo karma automatically. Transcend the mind completely, and from that point on, the karma is done. Karma is simply the habit of misidentification with thought, and the experiences that come as a result. The linear mind and karma are one and the same thing.

There is not a system of retribution built into the universe. It is our own faulty belief that, because we seem to have become separate from God, because we left the Kingdom of Heaven, we must be

Undo | Let go of Ego - let God
Easy God Out = Ego

punished. Once union with God becomes the permanent experience, there is no more accruing of individual karma. Freedom is gained, and one stops perpetually moving toward a future goal.

I will repeat it, the separation never happened. You only believe that it did. As the belief in punishment, separation and sin are surrendered, the direct experience of your own divine perfection dawns. When all action is in alignment with divine will, accruing karma, especially in a negative sense, becomes impossible. *yes*

107. What are the chakras?

The human nervous system is not just a physical thing. It exists as an energetic nervous system as well. A major part of that energetic system are the chakras. Chakra is a Sanskrit word that means, "wheel." The chakras are likened to wheels of energy that are overlaid along the physical spinal column. There are seven primary chakras that range from the base of the spine to the top, or crown of the head. Each chakra also relates to a major gland and organ, or organs, of the physical body.

The energy of life enters the physical domain through these centers, and creates the physical form. The chakras can be likened to portals, or gateways for life energy to enter the physical realm.

Each chakra resonates at a particular frequency, and so carries the energy of a particular level of experience. Stresses that accumulate through the various experiences of life, including those while in the womb, determine our outlook and attitude to the world in which we live, and to ourselves.

The base chakra, or root chakra, called Muladhara in Sanskrit, is the center that resonates to the experience of pure survival. It is the energy of the lower aspects of the human experience. This chakra is located at the base of the spine, and it is indeed our foundation. A balanced root chakra leads to an open and grounded state of being, and a harmony with the Earth. Stresses here tend to leave the individual with a fear-based outlook toward life, and a mistrust of the world and the people in it.

After the pure energy of survival of the first chakra, comes the realm of feelings, and of desire. The second chakra, which in Sanskrit is called Svadhisthana, is located a few inches above the base of the spine. It is at this level where the energy of feeling and desire enters, and it relates to the reproductive organs. Svadhisthana is the center of procreation, wanting and all worldly desires. When balanced, the experience of this center brings openness with emotion, and the ability to truly connect on that level with those around us. Stresses held here create the opposite; emotional defenses, jealousy, lust, and the belief that we need to have another outside of ourselves to complete us.

Above that comes the third chakra, Manipura, which is the center of personal will, the recognition of individual intention. This center is located in the solar plexus area, and is also very much linked to the vitality of the physical body. Functioning properly, there is a healthy self-awareness and a generous and happy outlook on life. A stressed third chakra brings about the need to control others, to be domineering and arrogant. The sense of self-worth needs to come from demanding the attention and recognition of others, and having them submit to your will.

Above that, in the middle of the chest, is the heart center, Anahata. This is where the lower three centers and their corresponding energies of individual physical striving, life and survival, meet the higher three centers of spiritual focus and intent. This fourth chakra is the heart center and relates to the energy called love. As it returns to proper functioning through releasing the stresses in the first three chakras, unconditional love becomes the motive force for life. This is love that is dependant upon nothing outside of you, and exists only to give and to serve. Stress and imbalance here create quite the opposite experience. Love is seen as limited and scarce, based on needing and taking.

In the hollow of the throat is the fifth chakra, Vishuddha, the resonance of spiritual will, personal divine power and creation of the individual reality. It is the power of speech and manifestation, and is literally the center of miracles. By surrendering the personal will to divine will, there is nothing that cannot be achieved. The healing of this center takes one from trying to bend the universe to one's personal force, which is always limited, and aligns life with the infinite, limitless power of the Divine.

In the center of the skull rests the sixth chakra, called Ajna, which is the center of divine or celestial perception, intuition and the experience of more subtle levels of existence. It relates to the pineal gland, the master gland of the body. When open and functioning naturally, linear thought is replaced by intuitive knowingness, even to the point of clairvoyance. There comes the recognition of the divinity of all things and the true, heavenly nature of what before appeared to be a purely physical existence.

The highest chakra relating to the physical body is the seventh, or crown chakra, called Sahasrara, which relates to the unity of the individual experience with the fullness of the Divine. It is the center that carries the resonance of union with God, the omnipresence of consciousness itself. It is the seat of truly omniscient wisdom. Fully opened, while physical life may continue on as it did before, the Self is clearly experienced in its fullness. The individual "me" is absorbed into the radiant totality of divinity.

Limiting impressions in the human mind directly influence how the energy of each chakra manifests in the individual life. The beliefs and judgments we give power to restrict, or enhance, the functioning of each center.

As one moves beyond the limiting patterns of those beliefs into a free state of awareness, the energy of each center is more able to move purely and unrestricted through the individual. The purity of the life force of the universe is able to move through the whole nervous system uninhibited, and so in all areas, life becomes quite miraculous.

The chakras are known in all cultures where there is a mystical tradition, not just in the East. They are the seven churches, or meeting places between man and God, that are mentioned in the Book of Revelation. The opening, or purifying, of each center is the opening of the seven seals mentioned in the same book.

It is not necessary to know about, or even experience the chakras, because simply by moving beyond the limitations of thinking-ness, all aspects of the self are purified and returned to their natural state of functioning.

108. What is Kundalini and does it relate to the chakras?

Kundalini is, again, a Sanskrit word, which describes the life force energy that moves through the nervous system. It is represented as a coiled snake slumbering in the root chakra located at the base of the spine.

In the Vedic mythology, this energy remains dormant until the individual reaches a level of spiritual ripeness, at which point it rises through the nervous system, activating each of the chakras and bringing about enlightenment.

In my experience, the energy is moving through the nervous system all the time. As it does so, the positions being held in any area of life become illuminated so we can see them and let them go, thus allowing the energy to move more freely. This can also be related purely to the experience of the mind. As the energy of pure creation moves through you, it collides with the beliefs and positions you hold on to and this creates the subjective experience of reality. The way to change that reality is to see the belief, judgment or position and let it go. Upon surrendering the thought, the energy of life is free to move without limitation.

Having said that, I never believed in the traditional description of kundalini and the chakras. I thought it was a nice analogy, but not accurate. One day I was teaching a meditation workshop for people who had been meditating for a while. Part of the weekend was dedicated to meditating together as a group for longer periods of time.

As I was sitting in the afternoon meditation session, I noticed a warmth beginning to emanate from the base of my spine. I noticed it, but then just went back to my meditation.

After a little while my attention was drawn back to the sensation. Then, without any stimulus from me, the experience was like warm honey being sucked through one of those children's straws that are bent into interesting shapes. It was like a three branched straw was shoved down my spine through the top of my head, and some cosmic being was drawing this hot, thick liquid through it.

The sensation slowly and continuously wound its way up my spine, or rather where my spine was located, up and up intersecting at the places where my chakras would be located.

As I noticed this energy rising towards my heart, and beyond, the last thought that went through my awareness was, "Holy shit, my kundalini is rising!"

As it passed my heart and moved rapidly up to the center of my skull, my whole awareness was blown out into a golden sea of consciousness.

I don't know how long it lasted, but two things became clear. The first and most important part was that even though it was a wonderful experience, it in no way impacted the silence of the true Self, which had already become a stable state. It was not necessary in terms of growth of consciousness; it was more of a by-product of it.

The second thing was that you just can't discount anything as a fairy tale!

Since then, the flow of the energy along the spine is constant. It varies in intensity, probably in direct relationship to my attention, and yet it is constant. Sometimes it moves out into the world of its own accord in different ways, sometimes it just moves on through. I don't know anything about it really, and don't care to. It is simply another experience arising in the infinite, silent field of awareness.

There are several practices that seek to force the raising of the kundalini energy. From my experience, it seems like when the relationship to the mind is righted enough, the kundalini is free to move as it will. Forcing energy has potential dangers because it could be made to rise before the individual is prepared, causing damage to the nervous system and mind, rather than healing.

The rising of the kundalini happens most safely as a result of letting go of negative programming. You may never experience it the way

I did, but that does not mean it has not happened. Like everything on the path to awakening, it is all very subjective.

If you are alive, your life energy is flowing, at least a little bit! Your chakras are functioning, at least a little bit. Let go of the limitations of your mind, discover the infinite silence of your own consciousness, and the rest takes care of itself.

If you lose your sense of a limited "me" in the boundless awareness of God, who cares whether or not your kundalini rises?

109. Is it true that the physical world is only an illusion?

I heard that a teacher once was giving a lecture on the illusion of the universe when he was run over by a bus! To adopt the belief that the world is an illusion won't serve you. To know that the universe is an illusion is not enough. Simply open yourself to discover who it is you are and you will discover many things about the nature of reality as your *own* experience.

Science is discovering just how illusory physical existence is; yet the implications for consciousness are virtually ignored. Begin with the step of discovering for your self whether the world is all there is. This journey is not really about whether the world is real or unreal, because it is both. Discover for yourself whether there is more to life than mere physical existence, and see where this leads you. It is important not to draw any absolute conclusions about anything. This just creates another line in the sand. To say, "this is how it is," is never accurate. You can only ever accurately say, "At the moment this is how it *appears* to be." Stay open to the possibility that there is always more.

The most important thing to hear is this…Yes it is possible to find all the data that points to the possibility that the world you experience is a creation of your own consciousness. That is one thing. A greater thing however, is that it is possible for you to have an ongoing experience of this; to know your self as the *source* of all experience. This is the invitation of eternity, and so few have ever accepted.

110. What about hope?

Hope is a very important aspect of growing from ignorance to freedom. At the lowest levels of human consciousness, there is no hope. To be confronted with seemingly insurmountable challenges and to have no hope is the platform for complete despair and fear.

As consciousness evolves, even though life may still be viewed as an impassable wall of challenge, there springs from within the hope that things can work out, that in some way everything is going to be better.

With that tiny glimmer of hope, we start to be more open to seeing the light that can lead us out of the darkness. For a while, hope is the only motivation to take another step.

Look at the example of a missing child. Even if the authorities have given up the search, even if society at large no longer believes in a positive outcome, the parents of the child will often never give up the search, always looking for the sign that will reunite them with their child. In these cases, it is hope that is the driving force to get out of bed everyday and do whatever it is possible to do. It is the driving force to continue to look for positivity when none appears to be present.

In smaller, but in reality no more insignificant ways, it is hope that leads people to search for spiritual truth. The reason why I went to so many different courses and teachings at one point in my life was the *hope* that this course would finally provide a way to experience what I had been longing for my entire life. Even when it did not, there was still the *hope* that the next one would.

Without that hope, I would never have continued to search, and so would not have found this teaching.

There comes a point though, in terms of the desire for freedom, where hope must be replaced by experience. When you discover something that truly brings you into the *experience* of the presence of peace and changes your relationship to the mind, hope is simply another way for the mind to pull you into the future. Hope is always about a future moment, you see? When you find a way to rest fully and completely in *this* moment, hope is no longer necessary.

From the experience of the fullness of now, hope is replaced by the innocent knowingness that each unfolding moment, no matter how it appears on the outside, is happening magically and perfectly. The tension of hoping that the next moment will somehow be better is replaced by your natural state of awe and wonder at the perfect unfolding of divinity.

111. Is it wrong to have 'worldly' desires?

While you have a mind you will have desires and preferences, but what is plaguing you is *attachment* to desires, or rather, the attachment to their fulfillment. What causes you suffering is not the desire, but the belief that attaining the thing or circumstance will make you happy. It won't.

As you discover your true self more and more fully, the experience that you are lacking anything, or need to be made more complete somehow is obliterated. You may notice a thought about desiring something, and that is okay, but whether you get it or not will not affect your experience one iota.

The desire thought arises from silence, moves through silence, and returns to silence. Your *relationship* to the appearance of that movement is the difference between heaven and hell.

Desire may be fulfilled or not, but your peace does not need to be affected either way. Freedom from desire is not whether desire thoughts appear in the mind, it is whether you grab that thought and believe that the fulfillment of that desire is necessary to be happy. This is what is meant by, "living in the world but not of it." This is also true renunciation.

Jesus said, "Renounce the world and the ways of the world." He wasn't saying ignore the world, he was saying see it for what it is. Don't get caught in the endless cycle of desire, chase, get, and desire again. This is the mind playing a game of self-improvement and this pattern will delay freedom forever until you see it, and let it go.

In virtually every spiritual tradition there is a fear at the presence of desire. This has lead to an idea that spirituality and a full life are incompatible. If a desire is fulfilled in some way, there is a sense of guilt in many students and a fear that they are moving away from God. Virtually everywhere, there is a belief in the righteousness of spiritual poverty.

I know these things from personal experience. The more consciousness evolved, the more the universe seemed to be moving to bring me a full life, but for a long time there was a belief that this was wrong somehow. Seeing these beliefs and letting them go has been the most freeing part of the entire journey.

It all comes down to attachment. You are not unholy simply because you have desires. What you seek is here and now, and nothing needs to be added or taken away. Your investment in the outcome is what keeps you separate from God. Surrender that, and life becomes richer than you can possibly imagine.

"Seek first the Kingdom of Heaven and all else shall be added unto you." Put your freedom first and see what happens. Most people will not do that. Freedom from limitation is always at least secondary to a great relationship, or a new car, or whatever, and it won't work like that. There is nothing wrong with having those things or even desiring to have those things, but the teaching is clear. Peace is here and now and nowhere else. Seek that above all else and life gets sweet quickly.

112. What is Samsara?

Samsara is a Sanskrit word referring to the endless cycle of birth, death and rebirth caused by karma. It is sometimes referred to as a wheel. It is the merry go round of mind created life after life, which is the reality of every soul believing itself to be separate from God.

Every belief in separation continues even after the death of the physical body. Time after time, the awareness is drawn to another physical experience that will provide the circumstances to transcend the individual limitations.

Many years ago I was meditating and I had a clear experience of the moment prior to the conception of this physical lifetime. There was a clear, non-dual state of awareness. Within that, there arose a subtle and almost transparent separate self. It was not a personality as such, more of a collection of wordless positions. At the same moment there was almost a sense of gravity, a pull beyond any ability to resist. As the experience became more and more condensed, it was apparent that there existed a physical conception happening that provided the perfect set of circumstances to transcend those positions. In that moment I knew everything about the life that I was being drawn to, and I knew everything that would happen would provide me the opportunity to wake up.

As I came out of the meditation, there was an absolute knowingness that everything in my life, and I mean everything, had occurred in perfection. All of the things I had judged as wrong and harmful had happened just as they needed to, and just as I knew that they would.

I picked up the phone immediately and called my parents. My mother answered and I thanked her for everything she and my father had done for me. I was overcome with gratitude. She tried to say that they had made mistakes, but I stopped her and told her that was not the case, that they had been the perfect parents. I don't think she understood, but it was such a powerful realization for me. The perfect unfolding of every single moment of life was crystal clear.

Once you awaken from the dream of separation and sin, the concept of samsara, of rebirth, of karma, of any form of separation at all, dissolves into the eternal light of God. Rebirth is over. There is no longer the need to unconsciously be drawn into a life experience to help you transcend a limiting set of positions. There may be a *conscious* choice to return to physicality to help wake up the rest of slumbering humanity, but in a personal sense, you have stepped off the wheel.

113. Is there any value in dream analysis?

It is not without value. For the most part, when we dream at night, our mind is experiencing the release of impressions and stresses that have accumulated throughout our lives. As we move into the sleep state, our body finally gets some amount of rest. It is in a restful state that the body gets the opportunity to heal and release stress. It is the mind's experience of this healing that produces the vast majority of our dreams.

From a therapeutic standpoint, analyzing your dreams can have some value, because you will see more clearly the process of your mind and the things that have impacted your life. I will be frank with you though, it is really not necessary.

In terms of growth of consciousness, there is very little value in analyzing your dreams. Your dreams are really just the experience in the mind of stress on the way out of your nervous system, so just let them go. Making a habit of analyzing the content of your dreams is not too different to having a good old rummage through your trash before you take it to the bin. Once you become aware of any experience, its value is over.

When you become aware of it, the underlying stress or impression has already released to whatever degree. Dreams are not too dissimilar to smoke rising off a fire. Once the position has burned, the smoke is merely a symptom of the burning having already occurred.

Is there ever anything to learn, or any messages in dreams? Of course there is. It has been my experience, and the experience of many people I know, that as awareness grows and there is less residual stress in the nervous system, any "messages" in dreams that are important become clearer.

114. Is there any value in past life analysis?

Not really. If it gives you a more distant or detached context to let go of something, then fine. It is important to realize that the pattern, position or judgment that is being surrendered is happening now, not in another lifetime. You have always had the same patterns, and the journey is to let them go so you can be free.

The fascinating thing about time is that it is a very subjective experience. Past and future are, in truth, happening simultaneously; it's all happening *now*. The apparent experience of a past life, or a future life for that matter, has value in that you can sometimes more clearly see a belief, or boundary, and so are able surrender it.

Looking for who you might have been in a past life is a waste of time, and a glorification of the ego. It is, more often than not, a tantalizing way to perpetuate the illusion of an individual self. Not many people want to remember being a mud collector or washerwoman during the French revolution, primarily because it is not much of an escape from their current life circumstances. Lots of people may remember being queen so-and-so, or a great warrior, or a disciple of a great teacher. Even if you believe you were Jesus himself in a past life, you wouldn't be the first! It has more to do with archetypes in consciousness than a real, individual experience. So many women I have met remember being Mary Magdalene. It is such a powerful archetype.

What appear to be memories may present themselves spontaneously, and again, it is all to be surrendered. Who knows where they come from? Most people don't even accurately remember *this* life, let alone some other incarnation. Analyzing *anything* ultimately becomes a waste of time.

I have had many of these kinds of experiences throughout my life. At one point they served because they motivated me on my path. They seemed to confirm that what I was doing was my purpose.

As my experience continued to grow, my perspective on the whole thing began to change. They are no longer *my* memories. It is all very impersonal really.

Whatever comes into your awareness, let it go. Right now you are already the fullness of your divinity. Far beyond the perspective of having lived before, died and been born again, you are infinite consciousness. What you are has never truly been born, and has never died. You are not subject to those things. You are immortality itself. As you remember that truth in *this* lifetime, you remember it forever.

115. What is the benefit of channeling or channeled material?

I read so much channeled material before I discovered the Ishayas. It all seemed so right to me at the time and I believed things simply because someone told me they came from an alien from another planet, or a master who had lived a long time ago. I even quit a job one time because I was told the aliens were going to land and make contact a few weeks later. They didn't, and so I was out looking for another job pretty quickly!

Most channeling isn't worth the paper it's written on because it actually delays the freedom of sincere seekers. There is some really good channeled material, such as *A Course in Miracles,* but it is few and far between.

The Teaching is the Teaching no matter what the source, and it is always about your true nature now. There is actually only one source, and the clearest channels know that. A rare few know they *are* that source.

Almost all channeling, no matter how well intended or beautiful in its delivery, is simply candy for the mind. In terms of waking up, most of it not only has no value, it can be actively misleading. Just because information is coming from an unseen realm does not mean that the source of it has your best interest at heart. This is the danger with channeling; you do *not* know the source of the material.

The human mind is fascinated with the prospect of the unseen. It loves psychics and fortune-tellers, channelers and soothsayers of all kinds. Unfortunately, there are unseen levels of existence just beyond the ability of the human senses to perceive, which are filled with entities that would love to have you deviate from the discovery of who and what you are. Even those entities that would love to help are not necessarily more conscious than you.

There is even material out there that actually advises the seeker to call in other entities to change and interfere with the nervous system. Nothing can interfere with you without your express permission. I would not actively invite an unseen entity to mess around with my nervous system, no matter how beautiful the promise of what would happen if I did.

If you have a disease in your body, would you ring a complete stranger for advice, or go to someone you can speak to and get an informed recommendation, someone who actually graduated as a doctor and didn't just buy a white coat and a set of good knives off the internet?

Every true Teacher is unwavering in the simple message that the Kingdom of Heaven is within all people equally. It is only our attachment to the world and the ways of the world, only our severe case of "I am the body-itis," that prevents us from experiencing it.

Whatever the apparent source, the true Teaching is the same. You already are that which you seek. There is nothing about you that needs to be fixed, added to, or changed in order for you to experience your birthright. Simply learn to surrender the identification with the mind, and reality will be revealed as it always has been. There is only one source of Truth. Speaking from there is true channeling.

116. What is a clear channel for God?

To be a clear channel for God, it is necessary only to get yourself out of the way. This is the purest form of what could be called channeling. It has nothing to do with speaking on behalf of some separate entity.

While we walk through our lives identified with thoughts and beliefs, we are constantly second guessing the Divine, which is trying to flow to and through us all the time. So few people even recognize an experience of intuition, or silent knowingness. So few people live in a spontaneous way.

As the internal limiting programs of control, fear and judgment are surrendered, automatically the qualities of intuition and spontaneity become more prominent. As love replaces fear, life becomes a more open, joyful and flowing experience.

To be completely free of the subtle fears and limitations of the mind is to live in perpetual peace. To live every moment identified only with the silent presence of your own being is to become a clear channel for God. Every area of life, no matter what form it takes then becomes a seamless flow of service to humanity. For this to be, it is necessary only to surrender the limited little will of the ego to the all encompassing will of the Divine. If you want to be a clear channel for God, get out of the way.

117. What is the Holy Spirit?

It is the perception of the Love of God in action. The Holy Spirit is the perception of the Divine calling you home. It could be likened to the feminine; forever receptive, non-invasive, simply awaiting your attention. Once one begins to realize that separation is not the natural state and the desire to unite with God becomes conscious, then the Holy Spirit also becomes apparent.

The Holy Spirit is actually your own true nature revealing itself in all things. It is not some separate part of the Divine; it *is* the Divine, pure and simple. It is the aspect of God that comes to the aid of those souls willing and able to release themselves from their own self-imposed bondage.

It is the recognition of beauty and Truth, and the acceptance of the invitation that these things naturally offer: To come home fully to your own birthright. In Sanskrit the Holy Spirit could be called *Ishani*. *Isha* means "Christ" and *ni* means "to lead." So, *Ishani*, the Holy Spirit, is that which leads to Christ, that which leads to awakening.

As one begins to open to the love that exists within, it is automatically reflected without. Life becomes filled with the qualities of your own inner state, and this perception is what is recognized as the Holy Spirit. Once recognized, it serves as a motivation to continue to surrender your self to God.

I have heard many people talk of the Holy Spirit as if it is something which is outside of them and beyond them, because it is not recognized as a reflection of the inner state. People will say, "I felt the Holy Spirit descend upon me," because, in a moment of openness to divine consciousness, the intensity of the experience seemed to come from a source other than within them. There is very little recognition of the inner surrender that occurred immediately prior to the experience. This is not a bad thing, because at least it fosters and deepens a commitment to God, as they perceive God to be.

The Holy Spirit is, in fact, the only thing that could really be likened to your soul. It is the part of your consciousness, the biggest part by the way, that still lives in absolute one-ness with the presence of God. When the tiny part of you that believes you left Heaven begins to turn back to face the sun of the Absolute, the light perceived is the Holy Spirit, calling you home, showing the way.

118. What exactly is the Grace of God or Divine Grace?

What is termed The Grace of God or Divine Grace is simply a recognition of something that was always happening; yet through ignorance, we blocked it, or more accurately we ignored it.

The entire universe has always existed to serve you, and primarily to serve you in your evolution in consciousness. As you begin to let go of control and devote your life to its true purpose, then you will notice how things magically appear to happen to support that. It can seem like a "Grace tap" has been turned on, but in truth you simply just got out of the way.

Once one prioritizes awakening above all else, it seems that magically, teachings or practices appear, or people show up in life that support that experience. Suddenly, things seem to line up to answer the inner call to come home.

This can seem like a new and exciting experience, but that has actually always been the case. Whilst you believe that life is about pain and suffering, the universe will support you in that. While you believe that all good things must come to an end, the universe will support you in that. While you believe that life has no point other than taking as much for yourself as you can before you die, the universe will support you in that.

Just so, once you decide that you are ready to dedicate your life to a higher truth, to walking in the footsteps of the Sages, the universe will support you in that, powerfully. This is Grace. To maintain a state of Grace, it is necessary to continually surrender more and more fully, to refine the focus to a point. This may sound hard, but it actually becomes easy, the most simple of things.

119. What is meant by "Judge not"?

Exactly that, let go of your judgments. It is only our judgments and beliefs that keep us separate from God. Our mind has divided the universe very conveniently into good and bad, right and wrong, this and that, me and you; all divisions. By seeing these divisions for what they are, you will automatically return to your natural state of simply experiencing. Some judgments are easier than others to let go of because they are more intimate to our sense of self. With practice, even these can be identified and surrendered and freedom is regained.

While it sounds easy to say, "Surrender judgments," it is in fact difficult to do it on your own without a good tool, technique or guidance.

Jesus was clear in everything he said. His whole public teaching was rooted in forgiveness. He didn't always blatantly say, "Forgive," but that is the essence of everything he taught to the masses. Whether it is another person, the world, or yourself that you are in judgment of, forgive it. In the forgiving, judgment is surrendered for a moment, and you move closer to realizing your freedom. It is not the forgiving that frees, it is the fact that it is impossible to forgive and judge simultaneously.

120. How can I let go of judgment when it seems to come up constantly?

So, judgment comes up. Then you have the automatic assumption that you are the source of the judgment and you tell yourself that you are getting nowhere because the same thoughts arise day after day. The first step is to allow the judgments to move through the mind without "grabbing" them and making it all a sign that you are not doing well. It is a self-violent loop to judge your self for having judgments.

The journey of consciousness is called expanding awareness for a reason. Becoming alert to the movement while remaining separate from it is everything. Get to a place where you *notice* judgment rather than *have* judgment and you are on the right track.

The last Maharishi of the Ishaya teaching, Sadashiva, was asked once if he still had judgments. His response was, "Judgments still flow through the mind." You could easily miss the profound teaching in this simple statement, but it is literally everything. Total detachment, non-identification with movement, not the eradication of movement, is freedom. Once you can allow anything to be there without identifying with it, you are free.

Believing that the content of your mind needs to stop, or to be different is the most insidious of all judgments because it keeps you trapped in the idea that you are not enough now. You believe that you are still at least just a moment away from Self-realization. All of your attention is on the thoughts, rather than the presence of your true nature.

The root cause of all human pain and suffering is ownership. This is *my* thought, this is *my* feeling and it isn't good. The only thing that can ever pull you away from the presence of God is the belief that what you are experiencing right now is not okay. If you can just for one moment simply be okay with whatever experience you are having right now, you will begin to experience more peace than you did a moment before. Once you see this, you can more and more easily allow your attention to be on that peace, rather than on all the things about yourself that need to be fixed first.

This is not to say that you allow totally idiotic behavior in the name of being okay with it, but once you can see the thoughts for what they are, and then there is no longer the need to act on them. You have created distance and righted the balance with the mind.

Everything in creation is constantly moving and changing and the mind is no different. For most of us, we believe that this one thing needs to change; that the mind needs to be stilled. Let it go. Allow your mind to do its thing and let yourself rest in something infinitely more beautiful.

While you believe that the thoughts in your head have the ability to stop you experiencing peace, they will. You need to see this for yourself. Discover who you are first and *then* deal with your mind, if you need to. Don't get caught in the trap that thought has the ability to keep you out of your peace. It doesn't.

121. Does my stressful past put me at a disadvantage for spiritual development?

No one is at a disadvantage in the dance to full awakening. In fact, those who have had stressful past experiences often gain freedom quickly because the contrast between the stress, and the desire to be free are so strong. Sometimes having had a relatively good and happy life promotes a lukewarm approach to union, which never works. Why would I want to change anything when everything is good? If relative happiness is what you want, then that's what you get.

This path is created absolutely by your willingness to surrender, that's it. One kind of past does not make the choice easier or more difficult, as the presence of God is eternal and equally available to all. Easy life, rough life, it all got you here. It is the choices that you make from now on that move you toward or away from what you want.

Either way, the choice is the same for everyone. Whatever your beliefs and judgments about reality, peace requires you to surrender them. Whatever your past, I promise, you can do this.

Start with *that* belief, the belief that your past inhibits your path. Right now, simply be open to the possibility that this is not true. Already there is lightness in you, and an inner opening. This is your direction. Simply be willing to begin. A great Teacher once said, "Simply begin and act as if it were so, and create your future ahead of you." The habits of the mind are familiar. Don't beat yourself up if they remain for a time; simply begin again, and again.

Your mind has limited strength. What you are aligning with has infinite power, limitless power. The very fact that you have asked this, the fact that you have begun, means that the recognition of your freedom is closer than you think. This transformation in you has already begun and so simply allow your self to remain open to it.

122. Gandhi said, "Be the change you wish to see in the world." Is this really practical?

What Gandhi said is absolutely true, but your question is about two different things. Gandhi's statement is pointing toward your inner reality, putting your own experience first. You asked the question from the perspective of impacting the outside world first.

The mind wants to point the finger to the outside to justify not choosing for the experience of peace now. "That's all very well and good, but what about things like world hunger and violence and crime?" What is not immediately apparent is that for all of history, mankind has tried to solve its problems by looking to the *effect*, that is, the external manifestation of the problem itself. This has gotten us collectively nowhere, and has actually kept us cycling around the same situations over and over again.

The mind will never believe this, but it is impossible to change anything permanently by focusing on the problem. Gandhi said the same thing that Jesus, and the same thing that Buddha, and what anyone who knew Truth has said. If you want peace, become peace. If you want love, become love; become what you want to see.

We have always seen the world through the looking glass of our own judgments. If you have internal patterns that tell you that the world is a scary, unsafe place, that is the kind of world you will inhabit. If you have internal patterns that tell you the world is infinitely loving and abundant, that is the kind of world you will inhabit. The world itself is not different, yet the experience of it is radically different; this is why life here offers such a swift opportunity to evolve in consciousness. No matter where you go or what you try to change, you will always be confronted with yourself.

Is it practical? As you evolve from fear and anger through to peace and joy, you begin to leave an increasingly powerful footprint in consciousness that affects all of creation. The consciousness of every human always impacts everything forever, but as one evolves more and more to be in alignment with the infinite, the impact one has is magnified immensely.

By fulfilling the purpose of your life and resting consciously in the presence of God, you impact all of creation forever, in ways that are indescribable. You affect real change. The benefit for you is that you immediately enter into the direct experience of true peace, you immediately begin to realize the divine perfection of all that is, exactly as it is. You find God, and you become that.

The benefit for everyone else is that the realization of that state becomes easier and more available for others. Each being that awakens leaves the doorway a little wider for those who will follow, and this is a life dedicated to service in the highest degree.

123. If God is everything and everything is perfect, then why is there so much pain and suffering in the world?

It is true that God is everywhere, but pain and suffering arise when that fact is ignored. Even if someone conceptually understands that God is everywhere, there is still the possibility of pain and suffering as this belief crashes up against what *appears* to be a more real experience. Only the recognition of the presence of God as a direct experience has the ability to eliminate the illusion of suffering.

We are so good at seeing places where we believe God has made mistakes. It is as if we believe that there is a big suggestion box somewhere in Heaven, and we have more than a few suggestions about where things could have been done better!

It doesn't work like that. As you expand in awareness, you will begin to see that all pain and suffering is rooted in the apparent separation from God. In order to discover for yourself if what is being said here is true, then you need to surrender your judgments about what is and is not broken in this world of yours. I say, "Yours," because your world is completely subjective, it is unique to you.

None of this means that one will not experience challenges, but all of our problems exist in the mind. All supposed problems exist in another time and place. Right here, right now you do not have a problem. That is why it seems such a contradiction that there can be suffering in a universe with God.

Our problems, our suffering are always somewhere God is not, and where God is, here and now, problems and suffering are not. As you walk this path you will see clearly that pain and suffering, Heaven and Hell, are subjective experiences brought on by your own choice.

The mind will point a finger to the outside to show you examples of suffering, but the stress you will see is within you, and transcending it is your choice. I am not saying that pain and suffering don't seem real and intense for the majority of humanity right now. What I *am* saying is that it is not necessary.

The change on a mass scale begins with individuals. It begins with you. To help all, it is necessary to help yourself, and so now the ball is in your court.

It is not necessary for you to believe this, or to understand it, but if you truly seek freedom, at some point you have to experience it.

The word God refers to the omnipresent source of all experience, including the world itself. Yet the appearance of pain and suffering of any kind is a direct result of identification with the mind or ego. Do not blame God for that which you yourself created.

What has been created by the mind can only be undone by going beyond the mind. You need to be ruthless enough that you are not willing to wait for the world to be fixed before you become free. It is the most common thing to want to heal everyone else before we heal ourselves. Many people actually feel guilty for finding peace because others are apparently still in bondage.

Ironically, it is by finding eternal peace within *you* that you will help to heal the world. Only by living in a different way can you truly help others. If you are unwilling, then you help no one.

124. Why does it seem as though there are so few enlightened beings?

It is true that there are few people who have reached enlightenment in comparison with the billions who live in suffering and separation. So far, these few have been enough to at least hold open the invitation and prevent the collective negativity of humanity from imploding itself.

Enlightenment is rare, but not because it is difficult. This is important to hear. In fact, it is the simplicity of the shift in perspective that makes it rare. All of our lives we are taught that if something is worthwhile it requires great effort, but in this endeavor nothing could be further from the truth.

When I began to search for truth, everything in my universe told me that there would be an arduous path to freedom requiring great effort and, in a twisted way, this was actually the way I wanted it. There was a huge part of me that still believed I needed to atone for my sins, to suffer to become worthy of God. When I found the Ishayas, the message of ultimate simplicity lit my heart up. I knew it was true, yet my belief in struggle was still in play for a long time.

I hear it constantly when I teach Ascension to people, "This is too simple; surely it must be harder than this." Yet within every single one of them there is the recognition that it is so, that simplicity is truth. When the belief in struggle arises, it is our choice whether we give it power or not. The most amazing part of awakening is that we can play it out any way we want to.

The possibility of enlightenment has not even entered into the awareness for the vast majority of people. Once enlightenment becomes entertained as a possibility, then all the support for that realization becomes apparent. The outcome is guaranteed because the seed of your birthright has germinated. Once begun it cannot be stopped, only delayed.

The realized Teacher must also wonder about the apparent scarcity of the truly ripe student. He or she stands as an open invitation to freedom, yet even if they have vast numbers of students, so few are ready to fully surrender everything, to make the goal of enlightenment their number one thing. It is easy to say you are fully committed to the goal, but another thing entirely to do it. Maybe there are apparently so few enlightened Teachers because there are so few ready students. When the student is ready the Teacher will appear, that is a universal truth.

125. Why does it seem like it is only men that are enlightened?

It only appears that way. There have been many enlightened women. Many of Christ's closest and most conscious students were women, and they became some of the greatest exponents of the teaching. They probably don't teach that in your church, but it's true.

It is not that women are rarely enlightened; it is because in the last period of human history, the accounts of their true roles have been filtered to the masses by a patriarchal society.

It's the same thing in the East. There have been many women who have woken up. Enlightenment is the most natural of states...it requires humility, surrender, receptivity. You have to allow for God, not force it. For most women, once this is seen to be true, the journey is easy and swift, as these are the natural qualities of the feminine.

The feminine consciousness is so important right now. It is so important for women to realize that they have a powerful role to play in humanity waking up. Imagine, the goddess stripped of her power for thousands of years, actually believing in the collective consciousness that she only has a support role in the greatest drama ever played out.

That's why the role of women has been so vehemently written out of the story, but that doesn't mean it isn't there. Anyone half awake can feel the depth of power in the archetypes of the Magdalene's, the Mary's, the Sita's and more.

The feminine role is Love and beauty and power. It is the intuition of the Holy Spirit and it is obvious. The divine feminine represents the Holy Spirit itself. There is no retribution needed against the male. You simply need to acknowledge your divinity and embrace it as a living experience. A wafer thin doubt is all that seems to cover it up. Doubting your intuition, doubting the possibility of union, doubting the magic that you are.

126. What happens to us when we die?

There are more than enough teachings on the planet that can tell you things about life after death, or what happens to us when we die.

This teaching is 100 percent about what happens *before* you die…this is about life *before* death.

So many people, the vast majority in fact, have never truly lived, and this is a tragedy. There is so much fear and limitation in humanity's experience that living is simply not an option. To be free of this is easy. To dedicate life to living is simple.

At some point, what happens after the death of the body will become apparent. We would want every single person to get to that point knowing that they did everything they came to this planet to do, to face death with a smile and leave this life with nothing undone.

Living under a mountain of "should" and "should not," "what if," "can't" and "what would they think?" is to miss the point of being born. The Kingdom of Heaven does not lie off in another realm waiting for you to die if you have been good enough. It is here and it is now. Experiencing this is the purpose of life.

127. What is evil?

That which denies the sovereignty of God best fits the term "evil." From the perspective of higher awareness, good and evil exist only in the mind. Jesus used the terms "ripe" and "unripe", not good and evil. It is only an unripe soul, one that is not ready or willing to remember its true nature that denies the reality of the Absolute.

As one "ripens," one moves back toward the qualities of love, forgiveness, compassion and courage and away from judgment, hatred, fear and separation. This ripening is natural and inevitable. True spiritual practice merely accelerates the ripening process. One recognizes and accepts divinity as a reality, and ultimately as the *only* reality.

At any moment in time however, there are those who will not only reject the Absolute, but will take conscious action to lead others away from it too. If there is such a thing as evil, this is it.

Once again, the idea of evil in a traditional sense is a lie. It is used to refer to the opposite of Good, to the opposite of God. That which is limitless can have no opposite. God has no opposite. Love has no opposite. The only possibility, other than having that as your direct experience, is to live in denial of that truth. Even the possibility of living in denial of truth does not have limitless life.

As one awakens to reality, it becomes clear that all is God, that all is Divine, and that the infinite power of consciousness cannot fail to return to full awareness of its own true nature.

128. Is there such a thing as sin?

Not the way it is usually interpreted. The idea that mankind has somehow done something to fall out of favor with God is not true. It sets up the belief that infinite love is angry with us, and we need to do something to atone for that. It is a lie.

Sin is simply the experience of separation from the Divine. It is not a punishment or some kind of eternal flaw in you, it is just the forgetting of your true nature. Atoning for sin is remembering your true nature, remembering your at-one-ment.

There is no punishment from the infinite for having forgotten, and upon remembering, the Absolute is not standing there at the doorway with its arms crossed, tapping its feet in disgust at your behavior. There is the recognition of boundless and completely unconditional love, and the absolute knowingness that you have never done anything wrong. Guilt dissolves, shame dissolves, judgment dissolves and what is left is eternally free.

129. How do the laws of manifestation help one along this path?

If viewed from the right perspective, they can help as an inspiration to surrender more control. You start to see that things are flowing a little more gracefully and it can be an inspiration to continue and intensify your commitment to the path. Ultimately, the laws of manifestation do not, in and of themselves, help you on the path; they are simply a by-product of it.

It is an exciting thing to entertain the possibility of consciously working with the laws of manifestation, but it sets up the potential for a lengthy distraction and even a detour from Self-realization. There is the possibility of claiming the *act* of manifestation for your self.

The ego believes it is capable of manifestation, the fruits of which are exciting. Very quickly it is easy to deify the ego, to begin to worship again at the altar of the mind.

I am not saying that playing with creating your reality is not a good thing, it is. It is necessary to be aware of the possibility that if the mind is seen to be creating all this great stuff, and I always wanted stuff, then the mind becomes God, and square one has been royally reclaimed.

A higher truth is that the universe has always existed to serve you. The laws of nature are constantly moving to bring you what you desire. Even so, the mighty forces of nature herself cannot keep up with the thousands and thousands of unclear and contradictory desires of waking state humanity. We say we want something, yet there are a myriad of unseen thoughts that are saying that we don't deserve it, or putting its manifestation somewhere off in the future.

You have to be clear on what it is that you want. Whatever it is, you have to be clear. There are no worthy and unworthy desires. There is no universal panel of experts judging and granting your desires based on merit. It helps to view the universe as absolutely obedient, but a little bit stupid...be clear. Once you are clear, commit. Give yourself 100 percent to what it is you want, whatever it is.

Ultimately, the root desire of all of humanity is the desire to be free. Jesus said it perfectly, of course, when he said, "Seek first the Kingdom of Heaven and all else will be added unto you." He did not recommend at all to "Seek first a nice car and a big bank balance and then look for Heaven later." He didn't even say, "Have fun, accumulate a bunch of toys and if you're good you can go to Heaven when you die."

He said to seek Heaven first, seek God first, and seek Freedom first. Seek your highest desire first and the universe will support that and every area of your life will be filled abundantly. You were born to live a full life, with passion and love and abundance of all kinds, but ultimately you need to get your priorities straight. Know what it is you truly desire most, and seek that first.

It is in the experience of expanding awareness that the response to desire becomes more rapid, to the point of being instant. Even beyond that, there is the experience of the universe responding before a desire or thought is even recognized. Once the minds split desires and beliefs in limitation are transcended, all flows in harmony with natural law.

The experience is exquisite, effortless, and completely impersonal. The constant key to discovering *all* of your potential is to continually surrender every experience back to its Source. The dance to freedom is a seamless allowing of God to give you everything, and the giving of everything back to God.

130. Why did God create a world of separation?

This is one of the ego's favorite traps for a spiritual seeker. The mind loves to find the cause of everything it sees as being wrong, and then point the finger at it. One of its targets is God. "Why did God do this to me? Why did God do this to them? Why should I want to unite with such a cruel thing?"

God did not create your world; it is the haven of your ego.

It is only the separated mind that sees imperfection and flaw. You live in a world, while seemingly the same as everyone else's, that is unique to you. It is your own mental filters of belief and judgment that create your experience of a life which is, in and of itself, benign.

All of the pain and suffering on this planet is created by the belief in separation from God. All of it is born from identification with the mind.

It is the seeming imperfection and flawed nature of the world that is actually a huge force for awakening. One will evolve to a point where, rather than bemoaning a cruel God for all the pain and suffering "out there," there is a direct knowingness that God can be nothing but Love. If this is true, then it becomes obvious that it is actually the individual perception that is flawed, and a way out is sought. Once the seeking has begun, the universe responds to bring what is needed to wake up from the dream.

131. What does it mean to be "addicted to the search?"

For many people on a spiritual path, the search is more important than the goal. It can be a badge of honor to be on a spiritual path. We go to workshop after workshop, spending untold amounts of money, inwardly marveling at the achievements of others or ourselves. We feel better and better with each certificate we attain, with each book we have read.

I always felt like I was getting somewhere when people would mention a teacher I had heard of, or a book I had read. It sounds funny, but it is actually the way many of us are. It takes a great level of maturity to get excited about actually letting go of the search and diving into the direct experience of the Self.

There is nothing more to look for, no more to achieve and nothing in it to gratify the ego. If I could, I would make a brochure for enlightenment saying, "You have everything to lose and nothing to gain!" There is nothing in this for the small you to show your friends or hang on your wall. There are no certificates for freedom, no levels where you will find yourself slightly above or below anyone else. Everything is here and now; All of it.

The attraction of the search is to be constantly putting absolute freedom off until another moment. The very idea of a spiritual path can be attractive to the mind. It is constantly holding the goal just a little farther off in the future, after just a little more improvement. This approach is like knowing that the possibility of union exists; yet still enjoying what the ego perceives to be the benefits of separation. This is control.

Is there more to be experienced? Forever, but now is the only moment when you can realize the presence of God.

When confronted with a Teaching that actually makes that the only choice, the reaction can be intense. The Ishayas' Ascension is such a Teaching. The most challenging thing about Ascension is the fact that it poses no challenge. A Teaching rooted in Praise, Gratitude and Love, and absolute simplicity, is the most offensive thing to some people.

Even in hearing about it, the mind knows that this practice means the end of its control. If you want freedom, you have to realize that the search is over. There is no separate "you" eternally struggling to return home; You never left, you just *believe* that you did.

132. Is Immortality really possible?

True immortality has nothing to do with keeping your physical body alive forever. It is possible to maintain the physical body until you *choose* to drop it, but choose to drop it you will at some point. I have met a lot of people who talk about immortality and with very few exceptions the desire to live forever is still motivated by the belief that they *are* the body, and their attachment to it. The desire for physical immortality is almost always rooted in a fear of death. Death is an impossibility.

Recognizing your own consciousness as eternal is true immortality. You are the universal constant. Throughout every experience that seems so transient, there is one factor which is constant...you.

We find ourselves frozen between two imaginary experiences called birth and death. I say imaginary because we are told that we were born on a certain day, or that death happens at some point, as if birth is your beginning and death is your ending, but that is not your actual experience. Both of those references are to the body.

Something is experiencing through the body, and that consciousness is you. The self you know now, if you cast back your attention, is the same self you were at 3, at 23, at 33, at 93 years old. The body changes around you, and yet you remain unchanging.

At 91 years old, my grandfather would laugh in slight frustration at the fact that he couldn't play tennis like he could as a youth. It was very clear to him that it was simply his body that would no longer do it, but he still felt the same.

Everyone has had these experiences. In those moments when you look in the mirror and wonder to yourself how you got to be so old, you are so close to waking up, I can't even tell you. You are face to face with the direct experience that you are not your body. This has happened to everyone numerous times in their lives. For one suspended instant you are looking at the real you.

In those moments immortality is staring you in the face, quite literally. Far from eluding you, you just turn away out of habit. We have become so attached to the body that we can't bear the fact that true glory is beyond it. Find the "I" that is unchanged, find it and stay there.

As the body ages it may become a bit stiffer than it was, or more wrinkly, but the "I" within remains unchanged. I am still as I was as a child, as a young adult, as a 35 year old; "I" am constant. In fact "I" am the only constant.

It is the most amazing thing really because it is the seeming imperfection of life, which we have created as a way of avoiding God, that is eventually the ticket out. At some point every being realizes, through some circumstance or another, that this physical existence can't be all there is.

That is what Prince Siddhartha did when he went outside the castle gates for the first time and saw suffering. He knew that physicality could not be all there was, that man's true nature must be more than suffering and death. He left his comfortable royal life and sat unmoving in his desire to know the Truth until he saw clearly the mind for what it was. He surrendered it, went beyond, and became the Buddha.

Immortality is not only possible, it is inevitable; in fact it is the only reality. Those who have gone before have left a very clear path, and very clear examples of what it is and how to achieve it. The degree to which we follow them is up to us, but follow we must.

EPILOGUE

The teaching of Ascension

Let me say right from the start that this book was not written as an extremely long advertisement. It would, however, be empty if it did not contain an invitation to the practice and spiritual path I have walked for over 14 years. That path is known as The Bright Path, and the practice is called Ascension.

Many years ago I was living and working in Melbourne, Australia. I was looking for something, although I didn't know what. There were two spiritual bookstores very close to where I lived, and I would go to them regularly for courses, meditation evenings, and to purchase books and magazines.

One afternoon on a day off from work, I went to my favorite little bookstore on Chapel Street. It was the beginning of the month and so many of my regular magazines would be out. I walked in and there was the new edition of *Eagles Wings*. I read it regularly and it was filled with all sorts of weird and wonderful tidbits.

I bought the magazine and went home to read it. As I flicked through the pages, there was an interview by one of the regular contributors to the magazine. It was the introduction to the article that grabbed my attention. It said something like, "I believe I have met a truly enlightened being…" That's not an exact quote, but it was something like that.

I started to read. The guy being interviewed was called M.S.I. He was talking about a teaching called Ascension. The interview covered a range of things, and really, the content was not that important. I had heard much of what he was saying before, or at least many very similar things. This was different in a very major way. It was like his consciousness was reaching out of the page to me. It wasn't just information that I thought was good; it was as if I could feel his experience. I knew he was the real thing.

When he mentioned the Ishayas, and the teaching of Ascension, every cell in my body came alive with remembering. I started to cry, to deeply sob actually. I felt like a huge invisible hand was squeezing the pain out of my soul.

What I didn't see, in the midst of my emotional release, was the part of the article that mentioned courses where you could actually learn the practice of Ascension. I did see that M.S.I mentioned that the Ishayas originated in India, and so I called my friend Michael, and told him about what I had read. I told him we had to go to India and find the Ishayas.

Several weeks later Michael called me and asked, "What was the name of that group you mentioned, the Ishayas?"

"That's them." I responded.

"Well," he said, "Guess what? They're in Melbourne and they're teaching a course of Ascension, and it's a five minute walk from your house!"

And so we went. The course was a Friday, Saturday and Sunday. Friday evening Michael and I were sitting in the upstairs room of another spiritual bookstore with over thirty other people, eagerly awaiting the beginning of the course. The Ishayas came out and sat in front of the group. They were both women, dressed all in white, and the first thing I noticed was the light in their eyes. There was a serenity and peace in their presence, and a definite *something* that I just couldn't place in their eyes.

The evening got underway. It was very relaxed and easy. After a little while we got the point where they shared with us the first Ascension technique. The technique is based on Praise, and they talked for a while about what that was and the power of it to transform consciousness. Then they wrote the words of the technique on the whiteboard at the front of the room.

When I saw it I almost cried. It seemed too simple. "Another empty promise." I thought. Then they gave us instruction on how to use the technique, and we closed our eyes to experience meditating, or Ascending, with it for a few minutes.

As soon as I used the Ascension technique, something marvelous occurred. My awareness was drawn into a completely silent, boundless space. There was no sense of a separate "me," only limitless presence.

The next thing I knew there was a gentle voice, which felt a million miles away, saying, "Slowly open your eyes." The two Ishayas were looking at me, smiling.

"How was that?" they asked me, knowingly.

"Holy shit!" I replied.

I knew I had found my path. I knew in that moment I had found everything I needed to return to the experience I had been chasing my entire life. Since that day, I have used Ascension continuously. The practice has never been stale, and has continued to expand and deepen the experience I have attempted to share in this book.

The practice of Ascension is simple and effective. It is based on Praise, Gratitude, Love and Compassion. It is completely mechanical, meaning it does not require any amount of belief. It can be practiced by anyone, of any background, race, age or sex.

The practice consists of four initial techniques, called Ascension Attitudes. Each one has a slightly different focus in terms of healing faulty beliefs. The first technique heals the judgments we carry in relation to our own subjective experience of life. It has the power to heal the belief that there is something wrong, thereby returning the awareness to the present moment.

The second technique, based on Gratitude, deals with the judgments we hold in relation to our objective, or physical experience. This includes the judgments we have around our bodies and our physical world.

The third technique, rooted in Love, heals the beliefs we carry about being unworthy of true love. This is key in waking up, because all of the delays and conditions we place on our freedom are rooted in the belief that we don't quite deserve it yet.

Rounding off the first group, or Sphere, of techniques is the Compassion technique. It rights the relationship we have with our own progress, and heals our relationship with the rest of humanity.

The benefits of regular Ascension are countless. It provides deep rest, allowing the physical body to release a lifetime of stress. It increases mental clarity and creativity. It brings an appreciation for the things in life that uplift us, and aligns the inner priorities with the upward spiraling currents of creation.

Ascension allows anyone who uses it to return awareness to the experience of the beauty of his or her true nature. It can be used with the eyes open as well as closed, and so provides a continual opportunity to choose for true peace.

Practiced regularly, along with the guidance the Ishayas provide, it can break the habit of unconscious thinking, and dissolve any pattern of limiting belief. If you allow it to do so, it will end the illusion of separation and return awareness to its natural state of union with the Divine. For those who follow the path to its conclusion, it will literally reveal the Kingdom of Heaven.

CONCLUSION

This book is intended to be more than just an entertaining or inspiring read. It is an invitation to remember that there is a divine purpose to your life. It is an invitation for as many people as possible to begin to remember who they are, so that all of humanity has the possibility to reclaim their birthright. Through the belief in separation and limitation, the Kingdom of Heaven has quite literally been stolen from us, and the path of return has been hidden.

Once you can see the simplicity of awakening from the dream of ignorance, then it becomes possible to do so, and quickly. Freedom from limitation is easy, and once experienced, every area of life becomes full.

When you are truly able to see the mind for what it is, you simply no longer entertain it, preferring instead the freedom of blissful awareness that lies beyond. Having transcended that structure, the same thing applies to all of the external limiting structures in the world; you simply stop playing.

There is no one who has power over you, unless you choose to give it to them. The structure of the world as it has existed up until now, is one that teaches you from the day you are born to obey an external authority out of fear of having your freedom taken from you in some way. As you awaken to your true nature, you will directly experience that your freedom is no one else's to give and no one else's to take away. It is this realization that ends all fear, and stops the ability of the few to control the many.

There is no need to fight and destroy a control system, whether it is internal, or seemingly external. You only need to see it for what it is, and let it go. Everything based in falsity will destroy itself; there is no other possible outcome.

So, remember who you are. Reclaim your divinity and live every moment of your life in freedom, joy and magic. You are a victim to nothing.

This is a pivotal time for humanity, if it wasn't, we would not be here. We are world healers, you and I. We are light bearers. We are way showers. It is now that you must remember that and show everyone what it means to be free. As you discover your infinite light, do not hide it. Do not pretend that suffering and limitation are real. If you do so, you help nobody.

If you are waiting for someone to save you, stop it. The savior the world has been waiting for is you.

Will most people reading this book take its invitation and awaken fully from their dream? No. The question is, will you?

Jai Isham Ishvaram

A B O U T   T H E   A U T H O R

Narain has been a teacher of meditation and consciousness for over fourteen years, and has taught in more than seventeen countries.

He currently resides in the mountains of north-eastern Spain with his wife and their very conscious dog.

For more information about the author, the book,
or the teaching of Ascension please visit

http://www.facebook.com/ChitHappens.books

www.thebrightpath.com

www.narainishaya.com

CPSIA information can be obtained at www.ICGtesting.com
Printed in the USA
LVOW07s0242071215

465712LV00001B/77/P